Biography

George M Johnson

When Blue Belonged To All Boys And None

RASHAD DOW

TABLE OF CONTENTS

TABLE OF CONTENTS

    CHAPTER 1
    TEETH AND TRUTH

    CHAPTER 2
    SAY IT LIKE ME

    CHAPTER 3
    HELLO, GEORGE

    CHAPTER 4
    BOYS DON'T JUMP ROPE

    CHAPTER 5
    THIS LAND, THIS LIE

    CHAPTER 6
    FLOAT OR FIGHT

    CHAPTER 7
    SHE LOVED ME DIFFERENTLY

    CHAPTER 8
    I SAW ME IN YOU

    CHAPTER 9
    CATCH THE BOY WITH THE FROG

    CHAPTER 10
    A SERMON IN NINE WORDS

    CHAPTER 11
    NO ONE ASKED, BUT I WAS WAITING

    CHAPTER 12
    ALL THREE WERE ME

    CHAPTER 13
    CROSSING, NOT CHASING

    CHAPTER 14
    THE FIRST TIME WAS MINE

    CHAPTER 15
    I BURIED KENNY, AND I WAS REBORN

CHAPTER 1
TEETH AND TRUTH

I was five when my teeth were knocked out. It was my first trauma.

But first, let me introduce myself: my name is Matthew Johnson. Actually, my name is George Matthew Johnson, but I didn't know that when I was five. However, in the end, everything will be important.

I'm from Plainfield, a little city in New Jersey roughly thirty miles from Manhattan's glittering lights. You could easily drive from one end of Plainfield to the other in under ten minutes. It's a compact city with many related stories. Triumph, sorrow, and trauma can all be found within those few square miles. It is a location I once despised but have come to cherish as my true home. My only home.

My family has been in this community for almost 50 years. My parents both worked in the city for about 30 years and continue to reside there today. My brother and I grew up middle class, or what Black people were taught to consider middle class. With Christmases filled with gifts under the tree, my younger brother and I never wanted anything. We were fortunate to have parents who understood what it was like to have the bare necessities and made certain that their children never experienced the same hardship. We are a rarity among most Black people, as we do not have intergenerational wealth like our white neighbors just one block away.

Family came first for us. Garrett, my brother and I grew up together at home. Our oldest brother, Gregory Jr., and sister, Tonya, from my father's first marriage, had already moved out. Plainfield was also home to cousins, aunts, and uncles. Holidays were usually large family affairs. For reference, I believe the movie Soul Food is the most similar to my background, except the violence. Maybe a little amount of fighting.

My parents both worked "9-5, 5-9" as we dubbed it. My father was a policeman who worked extremely long hours. My mother was the head of the police department's secretaries and also owned a hair salon in town, where she would go after work.

Some of my relatives used to live in Jersey City's projects, which my mother's mother, Nanny, said was unsuitable for the safe raising of young Black boys. Their parents were diametrically opposed. I recall their parents once paying a visit to Nanny's place. Aunt Cynthia and "Uncle" got into a dispute over laundry, which I subsequently discovered was really about drugs. It quickly evolved into a full-fledged fistfight in the upstairs corridor. It would be the last time I saw Aunt Cynthia in years. Nanny knew she didn't want her grandchildren to grow up in such an environment. As she put it, "Y'all can run the streets all you want, my grandkids will not." From that point forward, she took them in and enrolled them in Plainfield schools.

Nanny served as nanny, cook, nurse, and disciplinarian for us all. Nanny had brown skin and a full head of gray hair. She had a hefty build and one arm was slightly larger than the other owing to lymphedema. She was from Spartanburg, South Carolina, and despite having lived in Jersey for almost 35 years, she still maintained a strong Southern accent.

My family provided the type of upbringing and support structure that anyone would want for their children. The type of care, riches, and affection that should prevent a child from ever experiencing trauma or the same difficulties that earlier generations faced. Unfortunately, my life story demonstrates that no amount of money, love, or support will protect you from a culture that is determined to murder you because you are Black. Any community that has been indoctrinated that anyone who is not "straight" is dangerous poses a threat to LGBTQIAP+ individuals.

Because of a gap in the system and the fact that my birthday was a month after school began, the elementary school allowed me to begin kindergarten at age four. I recall having to "test in" to kindergarten because of it. So I was five when this event occurred (in the spring of the next year).

By that age, I knew I was different, even if I had the ability to express it or the maturity to properly comprehend what "different" meant. I wasn't into conventional boy things like sports, trucks, etc. I enjoyed baby dolls and doing hair. I could see that the feelings I was experiencing weren't "right" according to society's norms. On Valentine's Day, the males were meant to present their "crush" a card. I didn't want to give mine to a boy, so I gave it to a girl who was clearly a tomboy even at her age. I was always drawn to the company of boys.

As a little boy, I dreamed a lot. But in my dreams, I was always a girl. I used to daydream of having long hair and wearing gowns. And, looking back, it wasn't because I believed I was in the wrong body, but because I acted more female. I thought I could only be a female.

I struggled with being unable to express my whole individuality. One that would embrace all I enjoyed while remaining in the body of a male. However, I was mature enough to see that the only way I could find safety was to hide my genuine self, since, let's face it, kids can be cruel. However, I thought I had blended nicely. I was a world-class performer by the age of five, able to mix in with the boys and girls without anyone questioning my effeminate nature. Then again, we were so young—perhaps all the youngsters were just as naive as I was about the kids around them.

I was five when my teeth were knocked out. It was my first exposure to trauma, and now I'm ready to start there.

At that age, I wasn't allowed to walk home from school alone. So I walked home beside my older cousins, Little Rall and Rasul. During that time, my cousins lived with our grandmother, who also served as our primary babysitter because our parents worked long hours. Our daily schedule was walking to Nanny's house after school. I generally strolled with Little Rall, while Rasul led the way. Every day, we would take the back way, which entailed walking behind the school, through the football and baseball fields, and onto the street one block from Nanny's. On a regular day, the walk would take under ten minutes. Living so close to the school, I'm sure Nanny never dreamed that within only ten minutes, her grandchild's life would be forever changed.

The memory is vivid. I can remember smell the air from that day, which was sunny and warm like spring. That stroll to my grandmother's began as any other, with me holding hands with Rall as Rasul sped ahead of us. We were on the lawn of the corner house at Lansdowne and Marshall when we came across a group of neighborhood youngsters who I didn't recognize.

They had to be approximately the same age as my cousins—nine or 10 years. The main kid was Caucasian. Even today, when we discuss it, we use his full name, but I won't reveal it here. If I recall properly, the other youngsters were black and white. My cousins, I assumed, recognized who they were because they instantly began squabbling. When I sit with this recollection, there is silence. I can see it. When I write about it now, my body feels it. But once I closed my eyes to think about it, the situation became chaotic. I became terribly nervous. I merely clutched Rall's hand even tighter.

There were three of us and six of them, so it was actually two on six, because what does a five-year-old know about combat? The lads' arguing became more fierce, and my terror grew as they went closer to each other's faces. It's strange how close to home and safety one may be throughout some of life's most devastating events. I used to worry what might have occurred if we'd taken a different route that day or left school five minutes earlier. Would my life have turned out differently?

Before I knew it, the conversation turned into a battle, with me, the invisible boy, becoming the main target. As my cousins faced three of the boys, two others grabbed my arms and pinned me to the ground. I yelled for help because it was all I could do. The third child swung his leg and kicked my face. Then he pulled his leg back and kicked harder.

My teeth broke like glass on concrete. In that moment, I felt nothing. It was like everything was a dream. Then I felt pain. I also felt fury, which was a new sensation for me. I didn't really comprehend the feeling at the moment because I hadn't had the pleasure of experiencing it. The tears that flowed down my cheeks were no longer from anguish. I was now crying angry tears. Angry tears.

That wrath was enough to prevent the boy from delivering a third kick to my mouth. I broke away, lunged forward, and bit his leg with my remaining teeth. He shouted loudly as I bit through his jeans. By this point, my cousins had handled the other three males and witnessed what had occurred to me. They all ran toward us at the same time, forcing my attackers to escape. They seized my book bag and told me to "run to the house, Matt."

So I did. Ironically, this was the start of my track career, which I would continue from elementary to high school. At this time, sound has returned to memory. I can hear myself crying as I run home. I arrived at my grandmother's house and began to cry—my mouth was bloody, my lip was busted, and my baby teeth had been knocked out.

"What happened?" ", shouted Nanny.

"We got jumped," my cousins explained. Nanny went to get ice, wrapped it in a paper towel, and instructed me to hold it to my face.

It all becomes blurry after that, as I recall bits and pieces of what happened. My mother quickly left work to go to Nanny's. She sent an officer ahead to meet us at the residence and take the report. When my mother arrived, she immediately came to check on me. She sat in one of the dining room chairs and pulled me into her lap, wrapping her arms around me.

I finally calmed down when my mother held me. My uncles eventually showed up and sat with us. My cousins were still clearly upset. I sat in silence, feeling my mother's chest rise and fall with each breath. Police began asking my cousins what had happened, and they told their story. The officer instructed me to open my mouth so he could document the harm in his report. I recall not speaking for several hours after this occurred.

When I close my eyes now, I see everything as if I were having an out-of-body experience. I think about that day a lot. I wish I knew what prompted the attack. Could it have been because I was effeminate? Could it have been a racial issue, given that the main attacker was a white boy from another area of the neighborhood? Could it have simply been the harmful practices we teach boys about fighting and being men? I understand that impact and intent are always important, therefore even if their aim was not those things, the impact would change me forever.

There were no counselors or therapy sessions to assist me process what had happened. Therapy is still considered a taboo subject in the Black society. Those who are seen to have mental health concerns experience significant stigma and discrimination because mental health is frequently confused with mental illness. So, rather than having their child classified as something harmful, my parents did their best with what they knew.

We did what we usually did as a family: we loved on one other even more. My mother just hugged me in that moment, and we sat together for a long time. Eventually, she drove me home. But the next day was just that. The following day. What happened the day before had to be forgotten, or rather buried.

Unfortunately, one of the things I forgot was how to grin. I immediately felt self-conscious about smiling. Even as an adult, I've struggled to resolve this issue. Because my baby teeth had been knocked out, my adult teeth—almost "buck teeth"—came in quite early. Adult-sized teeth on a seven-year-old are strange-looking, and it drew me a new form of attention that I wasn't expecting. My lips protected the stolen smile. I refused to smile at each image. There are images of myself at seven, nine, thirteen, twenty-two, and twenty-nine years old in which I refuse to grin.

Every now and then, my mother finds a photo of me with my teeth showing. However, there are few. And sometimes they make me cringe. Other times, I've teared up, wondering if I was truly happy in that photo or if I just felt compelled to smile because someone said, "Smile, Matt," and I did. The fact that I don't feel pleased when I look at those photographs indicates that there was no happiness when I took them.

To others, did I appear to be a child who rarely smiled? Did they ever interpret it as an indication that I was coping with a trauma I couldn't overcome? Or did they dismiss it as a "boys will be boys" situation that I would eventually grow out of? To go years without smiling in images and rarely be asked why makes me wonder how many symptoms of trauma we overlook or neglect in Black children.

Black lads are expected to be rough and tough. To endure the pain without crying. If you get into a fight, you better win it or I'll beat your ass when you get home is a phrase I've heard far too many times from friends and relatives in my life. Being Black and LGBT poses various challenges. There may be fear of your own community and dread of being bullied by other children who do not appreciate your identity. When that kind of pressure builds up inside a young gay child, the anxiety constricts and can wrap you up in layers that become more harder to pull away as you get older.

As an adult, I have had to unlearn that my community's treatment of Black queer children is a byproduct of a system of assimilation to whiteness and respectability that forces Black people to fit into one mold in society, one in which being a man means being straight and masculine. I was unable to separate my Blackness from my queerness. The loss of my smile was a denial of both my Black and queer delight. I smiled as a coping tactic. My smile was a mask that concealed the agony of denying who I was.

Masking is a frequent coping strategy for Black queer boys. We bury the things that have happened to us, believing that they will not resurface later in our adult lives. Some of us are unaware that these hidden bones subconsciously guide our every movement and interaction throughout our lives. Surprisingly, many of us connect with one another via trauma and pain: wounded individuals seeking out other broken people in the hopes of helping one other.

I used to believe that if I took a decent picture of myself smiling, I would have overcome my feelings. But it only took one poor smiling photo to remind me how trauma has a strange way of appearing in our life when we least expect it. It could be an action that we dismiss as something else, while in reality it is the embodiment of a hurt we have refused to confront. A trauma that no one helped us fully process, or for which they lacked the abilities to recognize the need for assistance. Boys are not supposed to cry, so keep that garbage within. Sometimes to a grave.

There have been instances when I brushed my teeth too hard and got a taste of blood, which took me right back to that day. An adult crying in a bathroom mirror, pretending I didn't understand why.

Trauma appears throughout pop culture, frequently sung by the masses as a fiery song written by the singer to relieve that suffering. The entire community shares the trauma. Songs become our war cries; trauma becomes the glue that holds us together. So much so that I've heard people say, "I need sad Mary J. Blige to come back because her music is better." Our community struggles to connect with joy as much as it does with grief.

When I hear Cardi B say, "gotta bag and fixed [her] teeth," it's more than just a beautiful line in a great song. And, yeah, "Bodak Yellow" was a hit! But she is responding to years of hatred and criticism for having crooked teeth. She is discussing the trauma she experienced and what she was able to do to reclaim her agency in those moments and then utilize it to make others proud. Every time she talks about her teeth, she allows herself to go through the healing process rather than being burdened by the weight of holding the trauma inside.

For years, I carried that horrible event inside of me, and it was represented in hundreds of photos of my face without a grin. I tried smiling with my mouth closed and made faces. As I grew older, I'd get hit on by males and grin. They'd say, "You have a nice smile," and my first instinct was to roll my eyes in incredulity. And I'd even have people send me messages stating, "I noticed you don't ever smile." I'd deflect the comments with an excuse that had nothing to do with how I was feeling. I still had that five-year-old inside me who wasn't ready to smile. This queer part of me couldn't be fully expressed.

January 15, 2015, would mark a shift in my smile-related trauma. My mother suffered two brain aneurysms that day. It was a catastrophic scenario, and my family was completely unprepared. As a thirty-year-old, I understood I needed to keep it together. I was her eldest child, and I knew she would need me.

I recall the doctor stating, "It's time to return her to the prep room. My father and I decided that we would be the ones to walk her in. They wheeled her into the prep room just before you enter the OR and informed us, "You have one minute." My father stood on one side of her bed and I stood on the other. He leaned in and kissed her, and she responded, "I'm going to be fine."

I stood there. Nervous. Terrified. I finally kissed her, too. She noticed I was choking as I pushed away. I felt like the five-year-old youngster sitting on his mother's lap just after losing his teeth. And she, in her hour of need, was my consolation. It was as if she knew I had not moved on from that day. And before she entered the surgery room, she needed to ensure that I did. As tears streamed from both of my eyes, she glanced up at me and said, "Smile, Matt." "Just grin.

I offered her the largest smile I've had since the day I lost it.

My mother survived her surgery, and I learned an important lesson about holding on to trauma. It is critical that we undertake the work to unpack our junk. It's time for the world to allow queer Black lads air their grievances.

Smile, black boys.

CHAPTER 2
SAY IT LIKE ME

We lived in a ranch-style house with all rooms on the same level.

My brother and I shared a room next to my parents', at the end of a hallway. The third bedroom in our house was designated as a guest room in case anyone came to visit. When it wasn't full, we used it as additional storage space. My father is known as a "pack rat" because he never throws anything away. Unless he purchased anything new to replace something, he would prefer to preserve the old one "just in case." Most of the toys from my youth remain in the house, with my father explaining that "they might be worth something one day."

In our room, we had two wooden bunk beds—half of the year piled on top of each other, and the other half split apart on opposite corners of the room, precisely the way we preferred. There was one closet that had our toys and the majority of my grandmother's clothing from the previous thirty years—the one who lived in Virginia. As I previously stated, my father never tosses anything out.

We had separate dressers, mine tall and narrow and my brother's broad and wide, but we shared everything else in the room, even the television. We got along for the most part, so we never had any disagreements about what to watch. We were both getting ready for bed one evening when my mother shouted out to me from the living room.

She was sitting on the couch, waiting for me, watching television. We had televisions in each room. Another thing my father couldn't do without. As I approached her, she said, "Sit down, Matt." "I need to talk to you about something."

That "something" had evidently been building up at school for some weeks without my knowledge. She then inquired, "So, what is this word you have been using in class to talk to other kids?"

Here's some background information.

I was a very snarky young kid. The youngsters used to call me a sissy before they grew up and learned to say faggot. I remember watching women walk with a switch—that hip movement that goes side to side as you walk forward. I had a natural switch, but I knew I wasn't supposed to walk that way, so I did my best not to—emphasis on trying.

I was tiny and definitely didn't have hips. But back then, before other kids became harsh, I would try my hardest to fling my little body from side to side when I walked—even more than my natural walk did. My relatives would often say, "Stop switching, Matt!" But I kept laughing, even when someone instructed me to stop and walk "like a boy."

I was still in second grade—a joyful, talkative, but otherwise pleasant kid. I was thought to be intelligent based on all the standardized tests they required of us. I always appreciated receiving my scores and learning that I was "above the national average."

In terms of social life, I mostly hung out with girls. I gravitated toward them because they reflected how I was feeling on the inside. I imagined myself acting like them and imitating some of their mannerisms. I was too young to question if my performance was innate or not—though I now realize I wasn't mimicking anyone. The bent wrists, stride, and sassiness were all reflections of my own image.

I'd want to dwell on that concept for a second. Even now, I have moments when I am unsure of my mannerisms, femininity, and other characteristics. Are they a result of mimicking the Black women in my life, or are they simply me, or a combination of the two? I understand that it doesn't matter. And that, regardless of how my demeanor appears, they are natural to me. I just want to think about how I become who I am.

My buddies and I would use terms and phrases like "hey, girl" and "chiiilld," which were only meant for adults, but we were kids pretending to be adults. We felt we could get away with it as long as we stayed out of the earshot of adults. One of my school classmates was a tall, plain white girl who was quite kind. As strange as it may sound, I adored her last name. It was called "Haudenschild." I wish I had such a fantastic surname.

Around the same time, I met someone fresh in my personal life. I say this as if I had a personal life as an eight-year-old, but a new adult was joining the household. She was dating my uncle Rall. Crystal was one of the most attractive, cool, and witty Black ladies I'd ever encountered. She always had manicured fingernails and wore her hair with blond and red accents. I believed she looked like singer Faith Evans. She also drove a White Cadillac.

She was always a pleasure to be around and would take me and my cousins out as she got to know the family. I called her Ms. Crystal at the time, but she later became Aunt Crystal. My uncle Rall and others knew her by her nickname, "Honey." Honey was an appropriate name for someone who was so cool. I'd quietly wonder what it would be like if my name was Honey, too. Of course, the entire time I was daydreaming, I was picturing myself as a girl and occasionally a woman.

I rarely, if ever, envisaged myself in daydreams as an older boy. In my daydreams, I could be whoever I wanted to be. I imagined myself as a girl or lady who resembled my mother, especially given our physical similarities. My mannerisms were influenced by her and the other ladies I grew up with, particularly my aunts.

But, in fact, I was still a boy. Although I lacked the ability to live as I did in my dreams, I had to make the most of my existing situation. I wanted to feel more like one of the girls, but I knew I couldn't use "girl lingo" without other kids reacting differently. Boys were expected to speak in one style. Girls were expected to communicate in another language. So I would try not to speak feminine jargon when I was around dudes, and vice versa. I was "code-switching" before I even realized what it was.

During a gossip session with a group of gals, I used the term "Honeychild" instead of just stating "girl!" or "child." The word just rolled off my tongue smoothly and with sass. The girls appeared surprised, and I knew why. I smiled, bent my small wrist in their direction, murmured "Honeychild" again, and finished the rest of my statement. Then one of them did the same, following my example. I had coined my first gay slang phrase, although I had no idea what being gay meant.

It wasn't until I was much older that I learned about "gay lingo." Shade and yaaassss are terms we frequently hear used on television or social media, particularly by people who are not LGBTQIAP+. Language that children like me were shunned for using. Lingo that gay children today are still stigmatized for using. However, straight people can comfortably use it out of context.

This language or slang was coined by "Black femmes," an umbrella term that includes Black trans women, Black queer males, nonbinary people, cishet Black women, and anyone else I may have overlooked. However, much of this history has been suppressed from individuals who identify as gay, allowing the myth that queer culture stems from imitating Black cishet women to proliferate. But this is not true. This erasure also gives the hetero community "a pass" for employing terminology that would frequently endanger LGBT people.

On that day, all three of us, including Haudenschild, began using the word. It was great to have my own lingo. It reminded me of the women in my mother's salon who used to gossip. I felt powerful and liberated.

For the next three weeks at school, we used "Honeychild" in both group and individual interactions. Although I mostly used the word with people I felt comfortable with, the other girls used it with everyone. Before shortly, the entire class, even the lads, was familiar with the term "Honeychild." The word, which was formerly common slang among friends, suddenly became a classroom term. The word quickly extended beyond our small classroom and into the homes of the children.

Adults began to worry why a boy would utter a term so "feminine." Unfortunately, children's creativity is frequently criticized when it fails to fulfill acceptable gender performance standards. That is, if this term had been coined by a woman, it would most likely not have received as much attention. However, the fact that "Honeychild" was conceived by a boy raised serious problems.

I'll be honest in this moment. I can only presume that my classmates' parents objected to the use of the word. It wasn't like they discussed it with me or my parents. But I've lived long enough to realize that today's grownups are still uncomfortable with males who engage in activities that are not deemed "masculine."

One of the parents complained to our teacher about their child using the word and where it came from. My instructor was concerned about the pupils' overall well-being, so she called my mother and asked if she could talk to me about not using the word anymore.

I sat on the couch with my mother that evening. "Mrs. P. says you invented the name 'Honeychild.' "What does it mean?"

So I explained to her that I used it to refer to guys and girls instead of their names.

"Well, they are saying that other kids are using the word and that it's become a class distraction, so you have to stop saying it."

When you are a unique youngster, there always appears to be "something." You can't switch, say that, or act like this. There is always something that needs to be removed—and with it, a bit of you. The fear of being so vulnerable again exceeds the satisfaction that comes with being yourself, so you decide to remove that something.

Language is fascinating, particularly as a child. Children have been known to invent their own words and languages to share among themselves, which is frequently regarded as harmless. However, in this case, my constructed language was viewed as a danger to masculinity—an ideal I was expected to uphold although I was too young to properly comprehend its meaning or even how to type it.

So the grownups in my life decided what masculinity looked like for me. It was also their obligation to guarantee that the person I was, this "sissy," did not have an impact on other children—as if being who I was would change who others were. But that's what they thought. My words posed a danger to their children's identity—the identity they thought they would have.

Nowadays, when I think of the name "Honeychild," I can sit back and laugh. Giggle at the idea that what was once a threat is now as routine as wearing socks every day. As I already indicated, gay jargon currently controls language in this society. I've seen the language that was previously used against me become marketed for millions to use, see, and enjoy.

Except for Black queers. Our use of exclusionary language is still being used against us—just as it was when I was a child. Our use of it makes us simpler to target. We are not permitted to live as we do in the culture that we continue to develop and create. We get to watch people that oppress us use our content without facing the same consequences we do.

I remember not being disturbed by "Honeychild," but also not fully comprehending it. I simply said, "Okay, Mommy," and she smiled. I went back to my room and completed preparing for bed. I never uttered the word again, but I'm aware of the anguish it caused since I've never forgotten it. Like I never forgot how I acquired my given name. Like, I'll never forget getting jumped as a tiny child in kindergarten. I just filed it away in my thoughts, thinking it would never reemerge.

That was the last time I made up any terminology for myself. I didn't truly shut down, but I knew it had to do with my femininity. The only time I was told I couldn't do something or chastised for it was when I was acting overly feminine.

Children remember. We keep both the happy and bad memories. Children are also burdened by their parents' worries as they try to steer them to match societal expectations. My parents shared this anxiety, and with good reason. As much as they certainly wanted to fight for my right to live "as I was," they were also aware of the dangers my sassiness may put me in.

Fortunately, they parented with my best interests in mind, rather than their possible humiliation at parenting a child like me. They sometimes parented out of fear, knowing they couldn't protect me after I left the house. Most likely, there was a combination of everything. They never tried to "beat the gay out of me," despite knowing I was gay from an early age. They struggled with what they knew.

Later that night, I concluded that the only place I could truly feel safe was in my imagination. My ability to be a child was at the expense of my gender identity. The suppression continued that day. When I wanted to cry, laughter would drown it. A phony closed-lip smile would be used to mask the anguish I was experiencing due to my inability to be myself. That was the first day I started wearing the mask. The mask would cover my face, preventing anyone from seeing who I truly was.

CHAPTER 3
HELLO, GEORGE

The tall yellow house on Lansdowne Terrace in Plainfield served as my second home. We used to refer to it as the "Big House," in contrast to my parents' much smaller abode. This was Nanny's house, and we came here every day after a long, exhausting day at primary school. With my parents working, my brother and I would go there after school every day about 3 p.m. to 9 p.m. My mother would then come and pick us up after her time at the salon and drive us home.

The Big House was always entertaining because it housed my cousins Rall and Rasul, and my aunt Munch (when not in college). When I was a youngster, Nanny's house felt like "home." My mother would often ask if we wanted to come home or spend the weekend there. My younger brother and I always chose to remain for the weekend, which I'm sure our mother liked since she worked at her salon on Saturdays.

The Big House also represented family. There was a large dining room table, and Nanny enjoyed cooking on Sundays and hosting all of the Elders—Mom and Nanny's side of the family—for dinner while watching football on the big-screen TV in the living room.

I recall one Sunday evening when my cousin Little Rall and I were taunting each other, as we normally did. The jokes began out quite mild.

"That's why you're short," I remember saying to him.

"That's why you're ugly," he said.

Everyone let it happen since it appeared innocent at first; no one's feelings would be hurt. But everything changed quickly when I joked about his grades. For context, I was a straight-A student—a nerd by conventional definitions. My cousins were aware of my intelligence, and they were frustrated rather than envy. See, I was always held to the highest bar for how everyone else's grades should have been. So I said this:

"That's why you get bad grades."

This completely irritated him off. Fortunately for me, Little Rall was always my defender, so I wasn't concerned about him retaliating violently. Had Rasul been involved, the outcome would undoubtedly have been different. But instead of attacking me physically, Little Rall went below the belt and hit me in the worst way imaginable. With the fact that most of my relatives were not ready for me to learn, for whatever reason:

"THAT'S WHY YOUR REAL NAME IS GEORGE."

I stood there in disbelief at the statement. First, I thought, "What a ridiculous comeback." Second, I knew it was not true. So I told him, "No, it's not!" " He replied, "Yes, it is. Your name is George, not Matthew." This time, I became agitated and began yelling, "My name is Matthew, not George! " repeatedly until Nanny came from the kitchen into the dining room, where we were arguing.

"What's making all this noise? "

I looked at her and said, "Little Rall keeps saying my name is George, that it isn't Matthew." Her face hardened and her teeth clinched. She glanced at Little Rall with the expression that every Black child fears from their mother. That expression where you could see the words in their eyes before they said them: "I'm gonna beat your ass when everyone goes home." Fortunately for Little Rall, she could tell I was upset and chose to deal with him later.

"Come into the living room, Matt, and let's talk."

I sat on the couch with Nanny, who revealed that Little Rall was correct: my real name was George. I just remember sitting there wondering what that meant. So, was I expected to be another person? Was there a mistake when I was born? Did everyone else in the family use aliases?

I was devastated by the news. It felt as if my entire reality had been broken, and I couldn't understand what it all meant. I asked several inquiries, beginning with, "Why don't you use my true name? "

Everyone, take your seats. It's time for a narrative. Stories are a recurrent subject in this book, so grab some popcorn. Although I was never told why my family chose not to use my given name, they became more comfortable relaying the narrative as I grew older.

Back to the hospital room where I was born.

My parents and grandma were gathered around while they decided what I would be named. At the time, my father insisted that all of his sons' names begin with a G. My oldest brother, Gregory Girard Johnson Jr., was already a junior and named after my father. So, with all his inventiveness, my dad decided my name should be Girard Gregory Johnson. Did I mention my dad is from the country? You will understand why later. Fortunately, my mother and Nanny gave him an unequivocal "try again."

So my father chose to name me "George," after his father and brother. My grandfather's name was George Washington Johnson. It's alright to laugh, just like I did when I first heard it as a child. My father's brother was named George Stevenson Johnson. It's also fair to giggle at his name. The second effort at my name was to make me a junior under his brother, George Stevenson Johnson Jr., because my uncle had three daughters. My mother and Nanny offered him another "try again." Anyone who knows my father knows he is the king of his castle and has his own way of doing things. So, when all was said and done, they agreed: He could choose my first name as long as Nanny and my mother chose the middle one.

In that moment, Nanny took out her Bible and informed my mother, "This baby is going to have a biblical middle name, because there is no way in hell that I am calling a little baby George." As they thumbed through the chapters, "Matthew" struck a chord. They thought he was an excellent Bible character, and I reminded them of Matthew. George Matthew Johnson was born that day, though he did not stay in the hospital.

Returning to that night in the Big House, Nanny felt I was too young to hear that narrative, knowing it would only lead to more inquiries. So she offered me a general response, "We just decided to go with your middle name."

That night, my mother arrived to pick up me and my brother, and my grandma informed her of what had occurred. Mom asked if I was okay, and I said, "Yeah, I'm fine." But I wasn't. She said nothing more about it and drove us home. She had no idea it would be the end of my problems.

The next day, I went to school, and everything seemed OK. Mrs. P. called out the attendance as she did every day, going down the list of names to see who was absent from her roster. "Matthew Johnson," she stated aloud, and I replied, "Here." Class continued as usual that day. We had a quiz, and she allowed us 30 minutes to finish it.

"Pencils down, everyone," Mrs. P. announced as the timer chimed.

When she approached my desk, I handed her my document. She took a quick peek at it, then at me before returning her attention to the paper. It appeared that she was aware of what was going on but was unsure whether it should be handled in front of the class or privately. She said nothing at the time and went on to correct papers. Throughout the day, she distributed additional assignments for the English and scientific segments of class. Each time she gave us another paper, I completed my task and then wrote my name on top.

George Johnson

I never considered that the teacher could be concerned that I was experiencing an identity crisis. As a child, I adapted to change more faster than I ever did as an adult. I was able to transition from the night before, when I felt like my entire life had been a lie, to the next day, when I thought it was cool to have a different name. This easiness demonstrated my ability to simply go with the flow. I had agency—the ability to shape my own narrative—and this was a moment when I chose to do what I thought was best for me, no questions asked. As a child who rarely had the opportunity to choose his own route, in a society that demanded me to check off a specific box regarding my identity, this was one option I might consider. An identifying marker I could define.

I was eager to write my name any chance I had that day. I kept debating how I would make my G's. I was in my own little universe, telling all my mates my real name is George. For an eight-year-old, this was big news. Their acquaintance, who was formerly known as Matthew, was now known as George! The occurrence generated quite a stir, as other children naturally wanted to alter their names as well. I kept telling them that they needed to check with their parents first to gain permission, just like I did.

We walked to Nanny's house after school as usual, sat at the table, and started working on our homework. As soon as we finished, we headed upstairs to my cousins' room and started playing video games. We could hear the phone ringing, but we rarely received phone calls, so we rarely answered—unless Nanny yelled, "Get the damn phone." This time, she didn't, and I heard Nanny answer it herself in her regular white-lady accent, saying, "Hellooo." After a minute or two, she yelled for me.

"MATT!!! Come here and get the phone. It's your mom."

I ran into the foyer, where Nanny was standing. "Here, baby." She handed over the phone.

Hey, Matt. "I'd like to talk about the name you want to use," my mother remarked. "The teacher called home today and was concerned about you changing your name on all of your papers to George."

I remember assuring her, "Yes, I wrote it because it is my real name."

"I understand, but now you have a decision." You can go by George or Matthew. You can take your time making a decision. But you can't go back and forth, so we have to choose one." At that point, I became a little apprehensive. I was worried about disappointing them by choosing George over Matthew. Before I could say anything else, she responded, "No one will be upset with you for changing it. "You are old enough to make your own decision."

My mother always knew exactly what to tell me. She understood how crucial it was for me, even at the age of eight, to make this decision alone. One in which I initially had no say. I took a few seconds to think. Nanny was still standing there, waiting for my decision. Then I said, "I'm gonna keep Matthew."

"Okay, Matthew it is. I'll let your teacher know. I will see you later, okay? "

"Okay, Mommy!" "

And with that, my name was changed back to Matthew.

I was able to use the name Matthew throughout middle school, which was part of the public school system. In public school, they enabled me to use my middle name on all rosters. By ninth year, however, Matthew had failed to meet the high standards of my Catholic school.

On the first day of ninth grade, "George Johnson" was the legal name on the attendance roll, and no one was willing to change it to Matthew Johnson. There were a few kids at the Catholic school who had attended elementary and middle school with me. When they heard the name and my words "Here," they looked at me like, "Who the f*** is George?" it first week, I remember repeatedly stating, "Yes, that is my real name." Funny enough, my entire family was still against it. So I was called George at school all day, only to return home and be Matthew to my family, friends, and everyone else who knew me growing up.

Some have since called me George, while others call me Matthew. And, while I think this is a funnier story in the lexicon of my interesting life, I believe there is a deeper lesson here. This story is not my name. It's not about the shock of the eight-year-old who thought he was being duped, or the thirteen-year-old who had to accept using his first name.

This is about identity. This is about culture and how it determines what is a "good" or "bad" name, particularly in the Black community. This is about the politics of sex and gender, and we have the right to alter our names if our parents chose a name that makes us uncomfortable.

My mother supported my autonomy by letting me choose what worked best for me. But would the conversation have been as smooth if my name had been Dominique or Samantha? Even as a child, I understood that the name I used was for my family's comfort. That, while they didn't want to name a baby George, it would eventually be their decision to make. My name was meant only for me.

Going to a Catholic school where I couldn't use my "preferred name" taught me a good lesson about compliance. Besides wearing the same clothes, the school wanted us to follow a set of social and behavioral expectations. We were all required to attend Mass and take a religion lesson, regardless of our personal religious convictions. And we were disciplined for anything that challenged or did not meet any of those criteria. As rigorous as these standards were, they prepared me for situations later in life where I needed to achieve respectability criteria to be accepted. These conformist institutions did compel me to act out in various ways at school.

On one occasion, I donned a basketball headband on a dress-down day. I made it through three periods before a teacher informed me I had to remove it, which I resisted. She went on: "You are not allowed to wear that headband in my class."

"So, if I'm not taking it off, what's the next step? "I said.

In a smug tone, she continued, "I'm writing you up and assigning you detention."

"Okay, but this headband is staying on."

Agency—a phrase I didn't understand when I was younger—is a guiding principle that I wish we educated young children more about. Instead of responding, "You are wearing this," I wish more adults will ask, "What do you want to wear?" " And then have a discussion about those options. When we see our children not complying to social heterosexual standards or going toward objects of the "opposite gender," I'd like us to ask more in-depth inquiries about who they are.

Your name is one of the most crucial aspects of your identity. It is something that you possess. It is tied to everything you create. When you enter a room, your name commands attention. No two people sharing the same name are the same person. It is imperative that, like everything else in life, you come to value your name.

If you do not like your name, change it. It is yours, and it will be with you forever, so do with it as you like. As we continue to evolve in terms of sex and gender, many people will reclaim their power and alter their names, selecting names that reflect who they are rather than who society has shaped them to be. If you like your current name, keep it. But remember you don't have to.

The most important thing to understand is that you have the ability to make decisions that are in your best interests. The ability to fight back against society and even people in your own household. It is sad that we live in a world where asserting your agency may cause rejection, disdain, or even violence—especially for individuals who have known their gay identity since an early age.

Simply put, respect people for their names and how they want to identify. This also applies to honoring people and their preferred pronouns—he/him, she/her, they/them, god, goddess, or whatever. We are trained to believe those things should be the exception. People are entitled to use their preferred names and gender pronouns.

Allow yourself to unlearn all you thought you knew about yourself, and listen to what you need to know about others who live life outside the confines of a heterosexual framework. Most of you have probably never considered whether or not you like your name. If you didn't, consider whether you had the ability to change it. I hope you will now.

CHAPTER 4
BOYS DON'T JUMP ROPE

*F*ootball was the highlight of many boys' days.

Unless you're a boy named Matthew Johnson. I feared the idea of ever having to play football. My male classmates seemed like typical males to me. Like rough, tough, and shit-talking boys. But I wasn't. I've always seen these youngsters as a threat. The hyper-assertive, masculine, and dominant types. These types of boys made it plain that I was not like them. And when I wasn't afraid of these boys at school, I was constantly reminded of them at home.

My cousin Rasul and I did not get along well, and we frequently got into arguments at Nanny's place. He was a couple years older than me, therefore I never won one of them. It was clearly one of those "love-hate" relationships. We commonly talk about bullies at school, but rarely about them in our own families. He could be both my greatest protector and deadliest enemy.

By this point, I was in fifth grade and had realized that football was not my thing. For these and other reasons...

I decided to opt out.

Fortunately, we had several different activities to fill recess, which was everyone's favorite part of the day. For those who did not wish to play football, there was basketball. We had a full-length basketball court on black concrete near the pond near our school. It even had a side for the overflow kids who were eager to play the following game. The court also sat adjacent to the wide field where the other lads played football. And still...

I decided to opt out.

For those of us who didn't want to do either, there was a complete playground built on top of wooden chips. Our playground had been redone a few years ago with all new equipment, including a slide, swings, monkey bars, and balance beam. As youngsters, we created our own obstacle course, similar to the TV show American Gladiators, which many may not be familiar with. Think American Ninja Warrior, but roughly 20 years ago.

Two people would compete to see who could get to the slide first, run up it, and then descend the ladder. Next, climb up the monkey bars and swing to the other side, where you would jump down and walk the balancing beam. After the balance beam, you'd race through the swings to cross the finish line. I enjoyed doing this obstacle course in third and fourth grades. I was in fifth grade and...

I decided to opt out.

Fortunately for me, I discovered a new interest at recess. My excitement was expressed through the simultaneous turning of two jump ropes. One moves clockwise, the other counterclockwise. The ropes would hit the ground with the rhythm of a clock—tick, tock, tick, tock, tick, tock—until a person made a mistake hitting the rope or jumped out to give someone else their turn. Double-Dutching became my newfound daily freedom. It was my retreat.

We would leap from the top of the hill, overlooking the playground and the other children participating in various games. The hill was just above the field where most boys played soccer. The first time I went up there, the girls were anxious to teach me. I could already jump with one rope, having done so hundreds of times in gym class, but two ropes looked complex.

Sure enough, I was horrible at it. To begin with, I was concerned that there was no way I could get between the two ropes. My intellect was analytical and constantly attempting to figure things out. I couldn't handle jumping between two moving ropes. But I observed the girls leap in at various speeds and figure out how to get out without being touched by the ropes. I was sure I was going to do it. And one day, I did.

I jumped in.

This game appealed to my effeminate instincts. Double-Dutching was my technique of venting when I felt I couldn't be "sassy" in front of friends or family. That half-hour every day provided me with tranquility, and those ropes became more than simply a game.

It was me shifting between personas: the person I wanted to be on the inside and the person society expected me to be on the outside. My pride swelled with each misstep, each welt from the rope that slapped my legs. They were battle scars from the everyday effort I was putting in to improve my jump roping skills.

Around this time, as my grandmother would remark, girls began "developing"—or, more simply, growing breasts. So they'd jump into the ropes and keep their chests down. I'd giggle inside because they looked so foolish doing it, but it was their way of appreciating their progress, to be honest. Some girls had flat chests and held nothing. I'd mimic them. It helped me reconnect with my femininity and the person I daydreamed about.

I was the only kid who double-Dutched, so it was evident that this was not something boys should do. Better yet, boys lacked the room to do this without being mocked. Jumping rope should never have been a gender-specific exercise in the first place. However, the females didn't appear to mind my participation.

Jumping double Dutch was very girly, and there were so many great songs you could sing while doing it. When jumping with only one rope, this was our go-to song.

"Teddy, Teddy Bear,

Turn around.

Teddy Bear,

"Touch the ground."

Oh, but while we were double-Dutching, we usually went to my favorite, which you could nearly curse:

"Miss Lucy had a steamer,

The steamer had a bell. (Toot! Toot!)

Miss Lucy went to Heaven.

And the steamboat traveled to

"Hell-o, operator..."

If you made it through the song, you got to do Hot Pepper, which involved both turners turning as quickly as they could until you either jumped out or was whacked with the rope. We used to get so many welts on our arms and legs after recess from being whacked by those ropes. But we had a great time nonetheless.

One day, it became brutally evident that I could no longer juggle the identities. That a boy jumping rope, no matter how innocent, was not supposed to happen. Boys were expected to enjoy sports and dirt. Boys were expected to be friends with boys and have feelings on girls. They were not supposed to pretend to be girls. That day arrived far sooner than I had anticipated, and I made a decision that altered the course of my life forever.

It was a pleasant April day, and we were nearing the end of the school year. Lunch was always intriguing because I would sit with the lads and speak about "boy" topics, but then go to recess and spend time with my gals. Code-switching and navigating various venues was rather common.

Unfortunately, this day's recess would be very different. We were all dismissed from lunch and headed out the large double doors for recess. As usual, the youngsters proceeded to their appointed locations: the football field, the basketball court, and the playground with the wooden chips. Then there was me, minding my own way and heading up the hill to prepare for another day of double-Dutching.

We were ready to get started when a friend of mine named Todd arrived at the top of the hill from the football field. He tapped my shoulder and asked if he could speak with me for a moment, so we went away from the girls. Todd and I had been friends for a few years by this point. We collaborated on several academic projects and even had sleepovers. He was a white youngster at a predominantly Black school, yet he fit right in. People thought he was cool, and it was cool that he and I were buddies.

He told me the other boys had been chatting about me. I was used to the boys talking about me, but Todd coming to talk to me about it had to have been unpleasant. He told me that the other boys thought I wanted to be a girl, and that several of them referred to me as a "fag." Inside, I was burning, not from rage, but from terror. I'd witnessed enough disagreements and boys who weren't gay being called faggots, which usually resulted in fights. When you were called a faggot, you had to fight or flee—but walking away from the conflict was viewed as a sign of weakness and admission that you were gay.

My difficulty was that I was being called those slurs while having feminine features and engaging in activities that girls typically did. So for me, it would have to be about balancing those typically feminine attributes while also monitoring my safety as we got older. I knew that if I kept acting effeminately, the bullying would only worsen.

I despised being called a faggot. I experienced a physical reaction whenever I was called that word. My nerves went off. I knew I'd been called one before, but not to my face, so I dismissed it. This time, however, I couldn't.

As much as this was about me, it was also about Todd and others who liked to connect with me. "Birds of a feather flock together," so when they called me things like faggot, those who associated with me became involved as well. People who are straight who associate with me now, as adults, are still asked about their sexuality. Simply because they are my buddies. Adults who practice homophobia raise children who do the same.

Homophobia denies gay people happiness. I suppose that many LGBT people would like to participate in sports or other traditionally "masculine" activities, but they are afraid of engaging with people they do not trust. People who have stated unequivocally that LGBT people are not welcome, notwithstanding their talent. Homophobia is the reason why so many people who currently play sports are secretive—there is no possibility football, baseball, or basketball are 99.9 percent heterosexual.

We saw Michael Sam become one of the best college players in the game, only to be mocked for his sexuality. Dominant culture's failure to incorporate his queerness within a masculine-centered sport like football cost him a once-in-a-lifetime opportunity. It was not that he lacked talent. Sometimes you simply don't have the strength to carry the burden and complete the task. Navigating a space that calls into question your humanity is not truly living. It exists. We all deserve more than just being able to.

Todd offered a suggestion about how we could improve our condition. "You should play football with us today. Even if it's only for one day, it will get everyone to stop talking about you." I wish I could claim I had a different notion in my head than, "Do whatever it takes to make yourself feel better." For me, "okay" simply meant not being talked about. I recall looking at the girls and told them I would not be jumping with them that day.

I made the decision to opt out.

We walked back down the hill together to the field, where about fifteen boys were ready to begin the game. I knew who all the males were, and I was friends with a few of them, but not enough to feel comfortable. I remember being asked, "Have you ever played football? "

"Yeah, with my cousins," I replied. The moment was tense. It wasn't lost on me that I was now seeking acceptance from the same boys who had denied me the opportunity to do things I preferred, such as double-Dutching.

However, I struggled with not being accepted. I was also a skinny kid, and my relatives had moved on to middle school, so I didn't have them to wage this war with. This was a decision I made to ensure I could get through the days. Even if it meant pushing away the things I cherished. It was worth the fleeting sensation of being liked.

Oddly enough, I did participate in sports on weekends. My cousins would come to the same playground and teach me how to play basketball, baseball, and, most significantly, catch a football. I did those things with my cousins because they were enjoyable, not because I felt obligated.

This situation was about my need to survive. We got out there, and I was on offense alongside approximately seven other boys. The quarterback drew the play on the football, and we all left the huddle.

"Downnnn! "

He looked to the left. Then he looked to the right.

"Blue 42! ... Blue 42! ..."

"Set... HIKE!" "

I burst out of the formation like a rocket on a slant pattern, going up five steps before cutting out toward the sidelines. The ball was thrown to me, and I caught it. What transpired thereafter remains a mystery to me.

The first boy approached and attempted to assault me, but I remained standing. Then followed a second and a third. Before you knew it, I had three of them attempting to take me down, but I refused to go down. I dragged them all the way to the end zone that day. I didn't care how big they were; there was a spirit within me that wanted to prove I was just as tough—and better at their sports. The other youngsters were shocked, then excited.

My teammates rushed to me and we celebrated quickly. High fives and daps were exchanged before the ball was returned to the opposing team. Everyone commented on how "tough" I was. For me, it was one of the best days of elementary school. It was a time when I realized that not only was I an excellent athlete, but I could also utilize my talent to protect myself from bullying.

Football and basketball became my new interests. Although I finally came to enjoy such sports, the day I stopped jumping rope left me with a heavy heart. Even as a child, I learned that safety came first before satisfaction. I would often gaze back at the top of the hill, even as I tried to blend in with the other boys in the fields below.

It was interesting to finally feel like one of the guys. Hearing their chats about girls, the cussing, and the strong man persona. They discussed sex, although neither had really experienced it. Up until this point, I'd had a few male friends, but those friendships were primarily predicated on the fact that I had high grades and was kind of amusing in the shade. Now I had a reason the boys liked me.

I was never picked first or last at recess. This meant something to me. It meant people were looking past my femininity, which was a comfort, if only for a moment. Back then, it was either you sucked at the sport or people thought you weren't "manly" enough, or as manly as a guy could be. The arrogance of society to instill "manhood" in a child's life.

For years, I made do, but rather than settling on football as my ultimate sport, I discovered a new passion in track and field. It wasn't a really masculine sport, and I actually enjoyed jogging. I became very active in middle school athletics. Although we did not have an official team, we participated in a large track meet with all of the middle schools each year. The gym teachers were free to choose the best kids, and I was chosen both years.

I ended up running varsity for my final three years of high school. I was the team's leading hurdler, and in my senior year, I led us in scoring. I was pleased with it. I even had my name published in the papers once.

It was all deflection, though necessary. I would occasionally use athletics as a barrier avoiding discussions with my family about the elephant in the room. Instead of asking, "Are you dating?" "The inquiry was, "How is the track going?" "This is a much easier topic for me."

Finding happiness is crucial. To get there, you may need to push yourself beyond your limits. Even though my exposure to sports began with a fight or flight response, I believe it revealed some previously suppressed worries. It wasn't that I disliked athletics; it was more that I was afraid of dealing with individuals with whom I was uncomfortable. It explained why I like sports-themed video games but despised having to physically participate in them. Running track taught me that I could pursue a sport while remaining safe and true to myself.

As an adult Black queer person, I am now taunted because I enjoy sports. It's always been a running joke that gays don't participate in sports, which is false in most cases. I don't have to be bound to an identity that forces me to choose between two options. To do so would simply reward homophobia. I am good at football and double Dutch. I am still quite good at football and double Dutch. Most importantly, I am not bound by either. You don't need to be either.

CHAPTER 5
THIS LAND, THIS LIE

*C*ook School was a family fixture and a place for us to call home.

The Elders and Johnsons? We ran the school. We believed we did. Rall, Rasul, my younger brother, and I all traveled during the same years. Then there were my cousins Rick and Bernard, and numerous people who had previously attended Nanny's nursery. (Nanny was always caring for other people's children.) We were a band, and moved as one. We were taught that family defends family, therefore that is what we did.

I remember hallways being decorated with posters of historical figures. George Washington, Albert Einstein, Thomas Jefferson, and Benjamin Franklin were important parts of our education because they taught us about some of our country's finest brains and leaders.

Although my school had predominantly Black pupils, there were only a few Black faces on the hallway walls, including Martin Luther King Jr., Harriet Tubman, and Rosa Parks, who alternated with white historical figures. I remember thinking that all the "good" white and black figures were the same. Men like Jefferson and Washington were taught to us in a way that obscured the fact that they held slaves, yet Robert E. Lee was depicted in a very different light for supporting the same things. History has an amusing way of painting.

Although we were taught to admire and respect Abe Lincoln for liberating us from slavery, I never wondered why, a century later, Martin Luther King Jr. was still fighting for our civil rights.

Regardless of how much we concentrated on elder white faces in American history, there was always one period of year set out for us Black pupils. I recall the few white pupils we had always seeming out of place on February 1st. It was as if the tables had turned, and we were now the center of attention.

My K-12 education paralleled many other systems that oppressed the Black population, with Black children being taught by mostly white teachers. From the principal to the guidance counselor, we were surrounded by white authority figures at my elementary school. We had a small number of Black professors, but they were always the janitors, lunch ladies, and secretaries, which would be OK if they occupied positions of power. Obviously, none of those positions are incorrect, but it would have been preferable to have Black instructors and administrators. Being the "center of attention" allowed us to learn about others who looked like us for a change.

On January 31, the hallways were a mix of American history, including a few Black faces that everyone should be aware of. By the time we arrived at school on February 1, it seemed as if the ancestors had visited overnight and transformed the corridors into a tribute to Black history. You know how it feels when there's nothing under the tree on Christmas Eve and you wake up on Christmas Day to find it full of presents? It was Black History Month for us. Twenty-eight (or occasionally twenty-nine) consecutive days of Christmas.

Black History Month brought Black people joy. I felt great delight in learning about my past, as did the majority of the other pupils. I recall once when we had to study about a historical Black figure—I chose Malcolm X—and then cut up a brown paper bag to construct a waistcoat. On the vest, we were to put words and sentences about the person, such as crucial dates and data from their life narrative. We then stood in front of the class to introduce our "Black hero."

It made me feel like I may one day be well-known around the world, even though I had no idea what I would be recognized for. Thinking back, I've always had the notion that I'd be somebody. Not simply a banker or a lawyer, but someone whom everyone knew. It's a powerful reminder of how crucial it is for Black children to see themselves in the subjects and people they learn from. You may be unaware that you exist until you discover that someone similar to you previously existed.

But I only knew white teachers. Throughout my early school years, every teacher I had was white. Ms. Chiles and Mr. Robinson, the two Black teachers, were known for having "bad students." It's interesting that those classrooms were entirely made up of Black children. I suppose I was trained to remove myself from my family, just as straight kids were taught to separate from people like me. There are several levels of oppression.

Black History Month was always bittersweet since it seemed to come and go so swiftly. White history did not require a month; we were constantly learning about it. And because we had one instructor who taught multiple courses, we learned history every day, with a focus on how much the white forefathers contributed to the creation of the United States. I recall being equally enthused about white history since, at the time, it appeared to be my history as well.

And it was, but not in the way I was taught to think.

When I was in third grade, the school decided to present a play. It was themed "This Land Is Your Land" and featured bringing all of the students together as historical people from the past to demonstrate harmony across races. Fortunately for me, my queerness came over as theatrical, and I landed the lead role as Abraham Lincoln. I, a Black boy, got to play the sixteenth president of the United States, who liberated my people. It was a wonderful experience for me, and all my friends were equally enthusiastic.

At our school, the gym served as an auditorium. It had normal basketball court flooring and a platform in the back for events such as award presentations and spelling bees. That day, the gymnasium became my stage. Chairs were spread around the gym floor to accommodate the enormous gathering. It was showtime. Although I was scared, I knew my lines and was prepared to deliver them.

The show began with a representation of Thanksgiving. Back then, we were taught that everyone got along, even the American Indians and the Pilgrims. I have a poster image that was on the wall around Thanksgiving engraved in my mind. It depicted American Indians eating meals with the Pilgrims during the first Thanksgiving.

Takes a deep breath

It does not reveal that the Pilgrims stole the American Indians' food when they first arrived on the Mayflower because they were unprepared for winter. Many American Indians died due to diseases spread by white immigrants. "Peace" was frequently a survival measure.

exhales

American history is undoubtedly the greatest tale ever created.

The performance then soon progressed to the Revolutionary War and the early days of the United States. Black and white children dressed up as Washington, Franklin, Jefferson, and others to give speeches. There was a recreation of signing the Declaration of Independence and the Constitution.

Finally, to finish the show, I was to take center stage and read lines from the Emancipation Proclamation, although the play never mentioned slavery. I wore a jacket adorned with red, white, and blue glitter, a felt top hat, and a false beard. I also wore suspenders. I was the whole United States personification. After I finished, we all gathered to recite a poem in unison.

I recall how delighted I was in that moment. I was very proud to be playing the man who had done more for my people than any civil rights leader or president in history. I believe that part of the reason he was slain was his decision to free all enslaved people, allowing me to sit side by side with white kids and professors over 140 years later.

I used to defend Abraham Lincoln. I remember the teacher presenting us the quarter, nickel, dime, and penny. Showing how, on the first three coins, all of the presidents look to the left, whereas Lincoln's face looks to the right.

They almost seemed to be turning away from him.

He was assigned to the lowest and only color-coded denomination, copper. Abraham Lincoln was sold to me as a man who genuinely cared about Black people, and I don't recall a single Black student back then who didn't think highly of him.

In fourth grade, we were still learning American history. We were asked to research Paul Revere at some time. Paul Revere was famed for informing his fellow colonies about the approaching British troops, which sparked the Revolutionary War. Our teacher requested us to join groups and create a poem to depict the experience.

My bandmates had no idea I was a rapper. It's story time! I told you this book would be full of them, right? Uncle Rall, my mother's brother, was an actual rapper, however. He was known as the Raw Street Poet Rap Rall Supreme. He looked just like Rakim (google him up if you have to, but know that he is hip-hop royalty). We followed him throughout Jersey as he performed at shows and events. He even made a music video once. My older cousins, Rall and Rasul, could also truly rap. I suppose you could say that was in our DNA.

So, instead of doing a poetry, I had my group perform a rap. I wrote all the rap lyrics and taught them how to flow. There were two white boys in our group. I recall them struggling, but I and another Black child brought them up to speed. We moved to the front of the classroom, and my friend began beatboxing. I began—since I penned it: "Listen up closely and you will hear, the meaning of the story of Paul Revere."

We each had a verse, and then we all joined in for the chorus. When we finished, the entire class applauded us. The rap was so fantastic that the next day, our instructor made us travel from classroom to classroom and perform it for the entire school. Again, it was simple to honor white historical people at the time because we heard about them through the lens of their compassion for us all.

The intriguing thing about learning history is how much it changes depending on the school and the teacher. And it isn't always about how those teachers perceive history, but rather how they see you. And your position in history.

As I entered junior high, the history I had learned in elementary school began to unravel. Here, all of my teachers were Black, and the student body was predominantly Black. We began learning history that included slavery, and historical individuals such as Washington and Jefferson and their less-than-ideal histories. Our teachers wanted to make sure we understood what it meant to be Black in America. This occurred at the Ronald H. Brown School of Global Issues.

Ronald Brown was chairman of the Democratic National Committee in 1992, and he was instrumental in electing Bill Clinton to his first term as president. For this, he would be requested to join the president's cabinet as secretary of commerce, becoming the first African American to hold the position. It is critical that I express this since the white community has long obstructed Black advancement in all areas. Even today, the phrase "the first Black person to…" still holds significance.

It meant something when Halle Berry won the Best Actress Oscar— she is still the only Black woman to accomplish it. When Hattie McDaniel became the first Black woman to win Best Supporting

Actress, it was viewed as a step forward, but she required a special permit to enter a whites-only building to claim her Oscar due to Jim Crow-era segregation rules. It meant something when Barack Obama became the first Black president, 219 years after George Washington, a slave owner, became the first white president—or 145 years after Abraham Lincoln issued the Emancipation Proclamation. Symbolism gives people hope. But I've come to see that symbolism is a threat to true change—it allows people in power to say, "Look how far you've come," rather than acknowledging, "Look how long we've kept you from getting here."

Unfortunately, Ron Brown's life ended tragically while on a trade expedition in April 1996, when a jet carrying him and thirty-two people crashed into a Croatian mountainside. My city established a school in his honor. It was the least we could do for a "Black first" who would almost certainly be forgotten one day. Students had to apply and be approved despite it being a public school. Attending that school had a significant impact on both the pupils and the professors. The school's goal was to develop future leaders like Ron.

The administrators wanted to make sure they understood it. There was more emphasis on African American history than white American history. We learnt about slavery, but not simply as a CliffsNotes version of the Civil War. We learned about what our people had gone through and how those experiences continued to influence the culture we live in today.

We discovered that Abraham Lincoln was not all he was cracked up to be. We learnt about the Emancipation Proclamation, but we also read some of his words that were not included in the history books. They were insulting Black Americans and the battle for equality. The remarks that revealed why we needed Martin Luther King Jr., Malcolm X, Medgar Evers, and every other Black activist over a century later, since releasing slaves did not truly liberate us.

We discovered that Lincoln had many ideas that never made it into the pages of history books. To quote Kandi from The Real Housewives of Atlanta, my thoughts were "the LIES, the LIES, the LIES!" ":

"My primary goal in this struggle is to defend the Union, not to either save or eradicate slavery. If I could rescue the Union without freeing any slaves, I would do so; if I could save it by freeing all slaves, I would do so; and if I could save it by freeing some but leaving others alone, I would do the same."

"I will say in addition to this that there is a physical difference between the white and black races which I believe will forever forbid the two races living together on terms of social and political equality."

"And inasmuch as they cannot so live, while they do remain together there must be the position of superior and inferior, and I as much as any other man am in favor of having the superior position assigned to the white race."

"I will say then that I am not, nor ever have been, in favor of bringing about in any way the social and political equality of the white and black races."

"I have no intention, directly or indirectly, of interfering with the institution of slavery in the states where it exists. "I believe I have no legal right to do so, and I have no desire to do so."

Junior high was an intriguing time for me because I was actively denying my LGBT identity while still enjoying my Black identity. As a youngster, my Black identification made me more radical in my thinking and more eager to speak out against the whitewashing of Black history.

This type of parallel living was a regular source of struggle. To be Black and completely present, I've always felt compelled to push myself to be straight. To hide my tears, I wore my mask, which was full of smiles and laughter. A mask that many black people have worn.

"We wear the mask that grins and lies,

It conceals our cheeks and shades our eyes.

We pay this tribute to human guile.

With ripped and wounded hearts, we smile.

And speak with myriad intricacies."

Paul Laurence Dunbar created lines that resonated right to my soul. He was another of those heroes who received particular recognition during Black History Month. I wonder if those who taught us this literature were aware of how many children were actually experiencing it.

I left junior high with a completely different perspective on Black history and race in this nation. Even though I was only fourteen years old, I understood what it meant to be a Black "man" in the eyes of society. It was clear to me that beating Rodney King was racist. Or how divided the globe was shown to be with the letter O. J. Simpson verdict—which many in the Black community interpreted as a victory over a judicial system that rarely, if ever, allowed a Black man go free. Especially someone accused of killing a white woman. Abner Louima's case occurred in New York, and it made daily headlines where I resided. Four cops assaulted him and inserted a plunger into his rectum. Even as a teenager, I realized how difficult it may be for me to go from being a Black boy to a Black man.

Though my father was a cop, he understood that being his child would not shield me from how police behaved with Black guys. So my parents trained me early on how to behave so that you don't become a statistic. We call it "the talk" in Black families. Not about the birds and the bees, but about the hazards of associating with non-Black people, who will expect the worst of you as a Black lad.

My mother raised us to be pro-Black, which caused concern among other family members. The concern wasn't whether we'd be the next Angela Davis or Huey Newton, but if we'd be old enough to hear such terrible reality. I wish more parents did this, at least historically: ensuring that Black children return home to read Black literature and learn about their ancestry in depth. Because that is not something we are taught in school.

I recall Mom saying, "My children will know their history. You can't be so trusting of white people given your past." I never felt like my mother resented our traditional education. Rather, I believe she saw that we needed more. My father, who worked for a largely white police department, agreed with these thoughts.

My favorite of Nanny's stories was about her grandmother, Big Nanny. One night, the Klan showed up at her door, attempting to intimidate her and her family. Big Nanny took out her gun. Nanny always repeated the story about how Big Nanny could tell who was under the sheets because of their shoes. She had cleaned the shoes earlier that day; one of the white guys for whom she worked as a maid.

When you have that type of blood running through your veins, you realize that facing fear is in your DNA. I'd need all of that and more as I started high school.

Overnight, I moved from being in the majority of the student body to being in the minority. I was one of the few Black students at Bishop George Ahr High institution in Edison, New Jersey, a Catholic institution that was mostly white and Filipino. This shift in racial makeup occurred as I transitioned from public to private school. Not only did you need to have particular grades to get in, but you also needed a specific number of coins. Racism was prevalent at my high school, although mostly covert. I was never called a nigger, but I did get bizarre, racially tinged questions:

"Are you in the hood?" "

Is your family from the ghetto? "

"Is this your genuine hair? Can I touch it? "

What I was going through is called microaggression in academia. Simply explained, it is when someone attacks or undermines you only because you belong to a marginalized group. It's called "micro" because the person isn't explicitly calling you a n****, fa**, or both. Instead, they draw attention to your differences in a subtle way. Small actions may appear harmless or naive at first, but they can quickly become significant. These small beliefs accumulate to become a whole stereotype. This type of microaggressive behavior frequently results in overt racism or homophobia.

Sometimes it's purposeful, such as non-Black students asking harsh, insulting questions to rattle you. Sometimes, a person is unaware that they have insulted you or your culture. Remember that no matter how it comes at you, the impact is more important than the aim. You are not a laboratory rat on exhibit. If someone asks you a question and you have to squint your eyes and contort your face to ensure you heard them right, you've most likely experienced a microaggression.

My worst encounter with this occurred when I was in the tenth grade. We were in an American history class, going over the standard topics like Washington, Jefferson, and now slavery—because even when my high school decided to teach Black history outside of Black History Month, it only covered that one topic. Our syllabus ran from slavery to emancipation, the women's rights movement, the civil rights movement, and the final theme, "Look how far y'all have come." The only difference this time was that I was almost sixteen and had questions. As the teacher began to describe slavery, he referred to it as "a thing of its time," which I took problem with.

People frequently use the excuse "it was the norm" when discussing racism, homophobia, and other aspects of our history that they wish to avoid. Saying something was "a norm" in the past allows you to avoid dealing with the consequences in the present. It eliminates the notion that hatred ceases simply because a law or the passage of time has altered. People employ this argument because they are often unwilling to admit how full of phobias and -isms they are—or how much they benefit from social institutions that favor them.

This comment was no different, and it occurred in a classroom. My classroom! In high school, I was still outspoken and opinionated, and my friends and peers relied on me to say things others were too afraid to express.

I challenged my teacher hard on why he thought it was OK to simply state that slavery was "a thing of its time." Why didn't he recognize that people, white people, chose to enslave another race? Abolitionists and Quakers were able to recognize that it was wrong, so why couldn't all white people?

He reacted once more, stating, "There were numerous things back then that would not be acceptable now. I mean, if I had lived at that time, I probably would have owned slaves as well."

The classroom went silent.

I remember how surprised the white kids seemed. It wasn't what he said, but how he said it. So straightforward. I recall feeling heated. Like, angry hot. When I'm extremely upset, I generally weep, and I could feel myself approaching that point.

Thankfully, I had a buddy in the class who spoke out first about her concerns, but he didn't seem to hear her.

I eventually composed myself enough to respond. "That is not okay. It is not appropriate for you, as a teacher, to suggest that you would have had slaves." He continued to argue about it until concluding, "Let us just go on."

I was rarely afraid to speak in Catholic school. And I honestly don't know why, except that I believe that if I don't, who will? Perhaps it was a form of teenage rebellion, but it was more likely the beginnings of the activist I am today. When people ask how I got into activism, I typically respond, "The first person you are ever an activist for is yourself." If I wasn't going to fight for myself, who would? As a result, I became the voice for us all that day.

This environment was not like my public school, where we had school fights and students spoke back to professors who were not scared to confront them. My Catholic school's teachers valued politeness, and if something in the classroom made them feel "afraid," they would immediately call for security. It's no surprise that so many children of color and queer youth do not feel empowered to stand up for themselves. This double standard is known as the "school-to-prison pipeline" and highlights how Black children face higher penalties for the same offenses as white children. Back then, everything was as usual. To put it simply, when white kids spoke up, it was interpreted as nonthreatening, however when black kids spoke up, it was definitely perceived differently.

There are genuine reasons why Black children do not speak up, whether it is for personal safety or because they know it will be perceived as disrespectful if they question a white teacher or someone in authority. But it is critical to understand that if something concerns you severely, you have the right to challenge it. Only you can determine how far you are willing to go for yourself.

When I say Honest Abe lied to me, I mean that the history I cherished as a child was not the true history. I was taught that Lincoln and other white historical leaders played little to no involvement in the centuries of oppression that Black people have endured. When the media uses the term alt-history, it is a clear reference to what America has always been.

By the time I was a young adult, everything I had learned about white history as a youngster had been proven incorrect. The most important thing I learned from that change was to scrutinize anything that appeared to have a hole in it. If a story does not add together, do not be hesitant to ask probing questions. If people who are teaching you the material refuse to answer your questions, you must conduct your own research.

Being completely educated about your Blackness, queerness, and other aspects of your identity is the most powerful tool you can use to combat oppression.

In a world obsessed with telling you stories that are simply false, knowledge is your most powerful weapon.

CHAPTER 6
FLOAT OR FIGHT

The last day of school was always my favorite day of the year as a child. Aside from my birthday and Christmas, it signaled the end of homework, early mornings, tests, and worry. It was just enjoyable. Of course, because school is school, they still assigned me several novels to read throughout the summer, which I always saved until the last week of vacation.

Because my parents worked and I wasn't mature enough to be at home alone with Garrett as a preteen, they would send us to those dull Plainfield summer camps. The activities, rather than the workers, were uninteresting. We had reading and arts and crafts time, and every Friday we went to the zoo or the aquarium. Perhaps we weren't even bored with the activities. Perhaps it was because we had just finished nine months of structure at school and didn't want to jump right back into it.

These summer camps would last approximately half the summer. Later in the summer, we all became Nanny's duty once again. Rall and Rasul had become teenagers by this point, thus they were less visible. They'd acquired jobs, girlfriends, and were too busy to bother with me and Garrett all the time.

However, every year Nanny took all the grandchildren on summer vacation. One week away from Jersey and their parents. Just her and her grandchildren traveling across the country by air, train, or automobile. I truly miss those trips. I absolutely took them for granted.

Looking back, the trip to California was my best vacation she took us. For many of us, this was our first flight. We had only been in the air for six hours, but it felt like we had been there forever. We got to move seats, stare out the windows at the clouds, and disturb the majority of the passengers. We were headed to California to see my aunt Audrey, who also happens to be my and Garrett's godmother.

A specific California memory was spent in my aunt's swimming pool. My cousin Cierra, Rall and Rasul's stepsister, joined us on this trip. We were all together in the pool one afternoon. Despite wearing floaties, something caused Cierra to fear and believe she was drowning.

Little Rall swam up to assist her. As he tried to calm her down, she continued flailing—to the point that he was battling to stay afloat. Rasul and I noticed and swam out to the center of the pool, pushing them both to one side.

Until I started writing this book, I remembered the moment as funny. But now I realize that probably prompted my phobia of the sea. Following that day, when I went to children's pool parties, I would rarely enter or simply stay in the shallow end, away from all the other kids who could swim.

Our trip in California is one of my fondest memories because it was when my actual friendship with Nanny began. While we were shopping, she decided to get us all new sneakers for our trip to Disneyland the next day. In summer 1992 or 1993, Cross Colours was the most popular brand. All the kids had to have Cross Colours. Except for me.

My cousins knew they were getting the new Cross Colours as we walked through the sneaker store, and they were correct. When Nanny asked me if I wanted sneakers, I told her no.

"Well, what do you want?" Nanny asked.

"Cowboy boots."

My cousins looked at me like I had an extra eye on my face. But Nanny never flinched. She just waited and appraised the situation. Aunt Audrey asked, "Matt, are you sure you want cowboy boots?"

I voiced my preference again. "Yeah, I want some cowboy boots."

By now, my cousins were all attempting to save me from myself. They'd both taken their new Cross Colours out of the package and shoved them in my face, saying, "But, Matt, these are the sexiest sneakers out. "We can all look alike!" They were virtually pleading with me to acquire those shoes. Don't get me wrong, I liked them, but I was more drawn to cowboy boots.

At this point, I was clearly frustrated because I felt like no one was listening to me. "I don't want sneakers, I want cowboy boots." I was on the verge of crying. As you are aware, I cry when I am filled with wrath. But Nanny saw it and stated, without hesitation, "If Matt wants cowboy boots, we will get Matt cowboy boots. Audrey, please take us where we can get Matt some cowboy boots. I grinned immediately, and Nanny smiled back. They could occasionally coax a smile from me. And we all grabbed some cowboy boots.

When we arrived, the store was one of those Western-themed establishments. We were definitely the only Black folks in there. My cousins couldn't believe it, but my face brightened up the moment I walked in. I hurriedly looked around, and there they were: black boots with silver tips and white threading throughout. "I want these," I stated. They were the best I had ever seen. The silver tips were so bright, you could see your reflection in them. They were weird, but they fit me. They stood out and allowed me to express the aspects of me that were distinctive. I tried hard to fit in, but my spirit struggled harder to get out. This was my small way of getting it out.

Nanny approached the store clerk and asked him to acquire my boots in size three. He was a tall, white man with brown cowboy boots and a cowboy hat. It seemed as if he had stepped out of a Western picture.

He had a Southern accent and was quite friendly. I didn't want to take off my boots after trying them on. They were roughly calf-high, with a small heel that clacked when I moved. They felt absolutely great. They addressed both the boy and girl in me. Cowboys were macho, but the stiletto reminded me of my mother wearing heels. They represented the finest of both worlds.

However, Nanny insisted that I put my shoes back on so that I could wear my boots the next day. So I put my boots back in their box and took them out of the store, a grin on my face. The next day, I got to be the most embarrassed cousin as we walked through Disneyland, all dressed in the identical shirts and shorts—except they had new sneakers and I had cowboy boots. I was always supposed to stand out. I was thrilled that day, no matter how angry they were about how silly I looked.

Nanny planned to travel down the East Coast from Jersey to South Carolina in the summer of 1997, stopping in Virginia before arriving at Myrtle Beach.

This time, Garrett, Rall, Rasul, and my aunt Munch accompanied me. You never knew what to expect while on vacation with Nanny. We were always able to go shopping, visit all of the amusement parks, get up early, stay up late, and generally enjoy ourselves.

I remember her reminding us that we were fortunate because many children did not have such opportunities. Many children never leave their home state, or even their city. Nanny never wanted that for her children, and she definitely did not want that for us. She ensured that we not only had the opportunity to be children, but also had access to the same pleasures as our white classmates.

When we eventually arrived at Myrtle Beach, we all proceeded to the Pavilion to play games and walk the boardwalk. The next day's itinerary included miniature golf. Nanny and the boys got ready after lunch. Aunt Munch was the final person we waited for. So we waited. Half an hour. One hour. One and a half hours. It looked like it was two hours later when she finally emerged. We all chuckled since she didn't appear much different from before, but Aunt Munch was cool, smart, quirky, and always took her time. Nanny hated it.

We went miniature golfing that night and had a great time. We had a terrific time once we got beyond the first hole. I was up first, and this was my first time using a golf club. Now I assumed that what I watched on television was how I should swing a club in real life. Unfortunately, people around me were unprepared for my golfing abilities, particularly Aunt Munch's face. I took a hard swing like Tiger Woods and knocked her spectacles completely off her face.

She was upset at first, but quickly recovered and simply stated, "You don't have to do all that." I apologized and swung more gently the second time. When we returned to the hotel, it wasn't too late, and Nanny suggested we go to the hotel pool for a while because it was well-lit.

Rall, Rasul, and I strolled down to the pool and stood in the ten-foot deep end. Rall or Rasul asked, "Matt, do you still want to learn how to swim?" They were both excellent swimmers, and as big cousins, they wanted to ensure that I could also swim. I swear our upbringing was like a scenario from the film Stand by Me, but with four small Black boys playing the leads. Or is Family Guy a better reference? Regardless, it was always an adventure.

I looked at them and stupidly replied, "Yeah."

"Well, swim!"

Then there was a push. And suddenly there was a big splash. And there I was, coming up for air.

If your heart stopped, it's because something seems more hazardous than it is. First, I didn't know how to swim. It had been years since their California excursion. In pools, I either stayed in the shallow end or wore arm floats when I went near the deep end. This was a very real scenario, and I was terrified.

I was alone in 10 feet of water, and the two of them stood over me, watching. I panicked at first, but it wasn't long before I discovered I was still afloat. My will to not drown outweighed my fear of not knowing how to swim. I just continued kicking down and flailing up. I wasn't moving, yet I wasn't drowning.

After approximately 45 seconds, they both jumped in and started treading water next to me. They were smiling proudly, like big cousins. They eventually pulled me to the pool's edge, where I could catch my breath. One moved to the deep end, while the other remained at the shallow end. That night, they required me to swim back and forth across the deep end between them. They weren't worried about having a good time. It was more important to them that I could swim.

Back and forth I went, each time getting better and better, my dread diminishing with each paddle and my confidence building with each completed lap. As absurd as their teenage logic was (which I would never encourage), it worked. They pushed me into the ocean that night and stayed with me until I overcame one of my biggest fears.

It was late when we got out of the pool and returned to our hotel. I was overjoyed with my success, and they were, too. They taught me to swim in my own tough, tough style. But they were really teaching me how to fight for myself—with the reminder that they would always be there for me if I needed them.

They were always there for me throughout the most of my youth and early adolescence. When we were jumped, they fought till the end to protect me. Even after I received the cowboy boots, they didn't like them, but they would also dare anyone else to threaten their strange relative.

I could easily have drowned that night. Rose Hackman's Guardian piece on post-segregation public swimming pools discusses how Black children drown at around three times the rate of white children due to a lack of tangible and cultural resources, as well as racism. It's fascinating how many things in this nation white children take for granted while black children have struggled for centuries. Black people have long had a delicate relationship with water, and even a dread of it, dating back to their enslavement.

My forefathers were brought here on boats and stowed away in holds, unable to see anything. But they could hear water pounding on the hull outside. I think the last sound many of my forefathers heard was the rush of water. Even when the enslaved were able to break free from their chains, many decided to leap overboard and die at sea rather than remain in slavery.

Consider recent American history. Following the integration of public swimming pools, pools in largely Black communities were filled with cement or simply closed. This discouraged Black families from teaching their children to swim. This is the kind of societal sickness that runs through us. Find a fault, lack, or disadvantage in our community, and I can point to a system that oppressed and created it.

This is why I believe everything in our history is significant and has an impact on our future. Swimming was out of the question for me after watching my cousin almost drown. When I was older, I discovered that my mother nearly drowned and rarely goes near swimming pools. Which is most likely why mother didn't invest in our swimming lessons—she didn't see it as a necessity. Everything is interconnected, and it frequently takes someone breaking a stigma or practice to shift the destiny of a family.

Instead of giving up and sinking, I struggled to stay afloat. Much like I had done throughout my life up to that point, whenever I was shoved down, I climbed back up. Vacations with Nanny and her boys were usually a welcome break from the daily effort of being myself. It took me away from the environment in which I did not belong and transported me to a land of pure love. Love for who I was, without boundaries.

Every day when I wake up, it's like being shoved into that pool again. For almost thirty years, I've chosen to swim rather than drown. I know several Black and LGBT people who quit swimming because the waves were too rough and the water was too heavy. So many people were not provided the necessary education or safety to live.

The true question we must ask ourselves every day is, "Am I willing to swim?" Is this the day you drown? Often, we will have to make this decision ourselves. Unfortunately, in a society where Black queer people are still being killed on a daily basis, that decision is not always ours to make. But I swim nonetheless. Every morning, I put on my goggles and dive headfirst into racism, homophobia, and every other form of oppression that comes my way.

There don't appear to be enough Little Ralls, Rasuls, and Nannys in the world willing to reach into the sea and pull us to safety. Too many people remain silent when others in the community repress Black queer folks.

CHAPTER 7
SHE LOVED ME DIFFERENTLY

*L*ouise Kennedy Evans Elder was her full name. I always thought it

was funny that my grandmother had three surnames. To the outside world, she was all of those things, but to me and her other grandchildren, she was simply "Nanny."

As previously said, she stood approximately five feet five, was a touch heavyset, and had brown skin. According to the accounts, my grandmother's hair turned gray when she was sixteen, which I always thought was fantastic. Although she was the youngest of thirteen children, she was the matriarch of our entire family. When she set out to accomplish something, she succeeded. And if she couldn't do it herself, she would delegate it to one of her children or grandchildren. She was always terrific at delegating.

She was, and still is, the best cook I have ever known. She could create anything from scratch if she knew the components. One of my best memories of mom was being one of her kitchen workers for a Thanksgiving feast and seeing that she never used a measuring cup to make anything. She was making her famous sweet potato pies with me when I asked her, "Why don't you ever use a measuring cup?" How do you determine whether you've put too much or too little in the mix? " She laughed hard, then looked at me and said, "If you use a measuring cup, your food will taste measured. Taste your food while you cook it. This is where most individuals make blunders. "When you're done cooking, the shit will be nasty." We both laughed out loud.

She did interesting things like making breakfast for dinner, root beer floats, and handmade ice cream sandwiches. However, mom had to make mine slightly different from the other grandchildren's. She'd always microwave my ice cream for a few seconds to ensure it was soft. I was the kid who disliked when his food was either cold or too hot. Being a little different was the norm for me, but Mom never wavered in ensuring that I was adequately accommodated, just like the rest of her grandchildren. My Lord, I was weird. I have to giggle as I write this.

When we cousins discussed who her favorite grandchild was—because one cousin was usually quite sensitive about it—we did so primarily in jest with her present. I suppose it worried her that we thought she wasn't equal to the rest of us. After a while, she realized we were only joking, but her response to all the arguing about who her favorite was always the same:

"I adore all of my grandchildren, but I love each one differently. Because you all require various things.

The phrase "different things" spoke to my spirit.

It wasn't until I was older that I recognized what this meant, and how well mom loved all of us, even while she wasn't taking care of herself. To be honest, her entire life has been spent spreading herself so thin that she barely had anything left for herself when she went to bed each night. If we had known what we know now, we would not have allowed her to invest so much energy into us without reciprocating. More on that later.

Some of my relatives needed a place to live because their parents were going through a difficult time. Some of us needed a consistent atmosphere to return home to every day after school because our parents worked long shifts. Some grandchildren needed tough love and firm rules. She provided for all of us.

And then there's me.

A small queer Black youngster who was still unclear of his identity. I submerged myself in schoolwork, hiding behind my books. What I lacked in friendships, I always found in storytelling. While other kids were out playing with their own cliques, I was in the library, completing homework, or playing Jeopardy! On Nintendo. I enrolled in the Gifted & Talented program in third grade, which segregated the "smarter" students from those with average grades.

Education has a long history of being used to divide people in Black communities. W.E.B. Du Bois popularized "the talented tenth" idea, which held that the top ten percent of Black intellectuals will lead the remaining 90 percent out of tyranny. Although the segregation of people based on intelligence is not unique to the Black community, it takes on a different meaning when you know that white people, regardless of their academic performance, can achieve. Donald Trump rose from reality TV star to president of the United States. There will always be various standards for us.

When you are the smartest member of a Black family, your relatives want your advice on everything. It's practically a running joke in our society that you can go to college for one thing, but people will come to you for everything else because you're "the educated one." Even Nanny believed education was key. Her parents were not educated, so they did not impose it on her, and she, in turn, was not "book educated," so she made certain we took it seriously.

My grandma, knowing how smart I was, wanted to make me her protégé. See, Nanny was more than simply a caretaker and cook. She was a hustler. The concept of "the hustle" is frequently portrayed negatively in the mainstream media. What many of us in the Black community refer to as "hustling," is taught in college business schools as "multiple streams of income."

My grandmother maintained a nursery out of her house, where the majority of the local kids grew up. She also cooked pies and catered parties throughout the state. She was a registered nurse with an affluent white client in South Jersey, whom she visited twice a week. She also held flea markets and garage sales. Nanny understood how to save a check, money in the bank, and cash under the mattress for a rainy day.

I became her sidekick and business partner, participating in a variety of little companies. We once decided that I should establish a candy business to supplement my income for toys, clothes, and other necessities. We went to BJs and purchased the candy in bulk. First, she gave me a $100 loan. With that, I was able to purchase what she called my "stock." When we returned home, she made me calculate how many pieces I had, how much I needed to sell each item for, and how much profit I could earn. We agreed that I would repay the debt monthly, at twenty dollars per week, until it was paid off.

I sold candy to every youngster on the playground both before and after school. I made a cool hundred tossing Pop Rocks in the yard. The activity continued for months before the school noticed. It was not illegal to sell the sweets, but the parents complained that their children were "coming up short" on their lunch money every week.

For years my grandma and I were a team. Slinging Pop Rocks was only one of our many hustles. Every weekend, we'd go to the flea market early in the morning to sell old items from the house, such as china dolls or pies and cakes she'd made the night before. It became a weekly event. I enjoyed hanging out with her, bartering with potential purchasers, meeting new people, and getting out of the house. The days would be long, but enjoyable. She always made sure I had things to do. There was never a crisis she couldn't handle.

As a child, I didn't completely appreciate what it meant to spend time with her. I reflect on how valuable every minute I have with her is now, and how those minutes felt boundless back then. I never considered the day when she would no longer be in corporeal form. She was my grandmother, yes, but she was also my buddy. She gave me something to be proud of: the ability to serve others with less than I had. My skill to earn money.

Even in high school, she was always by my side. As freshman in Catholic school, we were all forced to complete 250 hours of community service each year. Coming from a public school where I had never seen such criteria, I had no idea how I was going to meet them. All of the white kids appeared to have internships or volunteer opportunities lined up to sign their hours away. My parents, who already paid $5,000 a year for the school, lacked the financial resources to take on this additional responsibility. But she did.

Rather than having me pick a random charity to work for, mother established the Sarah Marsh Missionary Society Soup Kitchen at Mt. Zion AME Church, where we had been members all our lives. She basically started a whole soup kitchen so I could complete my community service hours. Every Saturday morning, we went to church, occasionally with other church women, but often by ourselves. We would prepare soup and meals for the sick and shut-ins. Then, during midday, we would travel about the city, visiting and feeding church members. We would talk to each of them for a few minutes before moving on to the next location. We did this for four years, until Mom was confident I had completed enough hours to graduate from high school.

It wasn't until the end of high school that I realized what she was doing with all her hustle. It wasn't only that she thought I was brilliant and should learn how to make money. It wasn't only that she wanted me to be a loving individual who gave back to the community. She wanted me to be all of those things, but more importantly, she did not want me to be alone.

I was growing isolated about the age of ten, and she noticed it. I tried so hard to hide my queer identity and blend in, but I just couldn't. I had pals, but they were not like my cousins and brothers' friends. My elder cousins had friend groups, and I occasionally joined them. But I'd often be too young to hang with them. They would go to parties and the neighborhood pool together, and they would frequently fight with other groups. They were a close unit, but not my unit.

My younger brother had a full staff as well. When they were younger, they all had the same sneakers. They all joined the same sports leagues so they could socialize together. They attended elementary, middle, and high school together. Even as adults, they all live in Plainfield, serve as godparents for each other's children, and meet on a weekly basis. My brother was the leader then and now.

I had my books.

I had homework.

I had myself, yet I was isolated.

My grandma frequently prioritized me over herself, as she was a natural caregiver. She wasn't going to leave me alone, even if it meant carrying a tiny child everywhere she went. Nanny decided to be my circle. She was my best buddy whenever I needed one. I recall hundreds of times when she would play Rummy 500 with me for hours until I was ready to sleep. It's seven a.m. "Let's roll" throughout the state to see the flea markets. We were in this together. Furthermore, she had already experienced it with youngsters in our family, including myself.

Growing up, I had a transsexual cousin, Hope, and several lesbians and gays in my family. My grandma watched Hope grow and transition, which I believe helped her understand what she saw in me. She had also witnessed the harm that occurs when children who are "different" are not nurtured and cherished in the same manner as other children are. When she says, "I love each of you differently," she does not imply I love you less. Rather, she means I love you whole and exactly as you are.

I frequently wonder what it would be like if every household had a "Nanny" in it. Why was my Black queer experience one of unconditional love while others have become symbols of hatred and familial violence? Although the national rate of homelessness for LGBTQIAP+ youth is approaching 40%, the rate in my family has always been zero percent. How could one family get it right while the rest of the world has gone so wrong? We should have followed the rule. Not an exception.

Instead, the guideline resembles "I'd rather have a dead child than a gay child." Baby Giovanni Melton's father allegedly maintained this thinking after killing his son on November 2, 2017. My father never said anything about how feminine I was. My mother, who understood all along, established a family support structure for me when I was two. She realized that later in life, I would need individuals who could connect to my experience—aunts and uncles who loved me, loved me, and loved me even more. Cousins who were always eager to battle for me, and siblings who have always supported me.

Family relationships are a commonly discussed topic in LGBTQIAP+ culture. "Created family" is a system in which friends from many walks of life form highly close friendship circles in an effort to provide a familial setting for those who are not welcomed at home.

Our culture has always found a way to provide shelter and refuge where none existed. The television program Pose truly illustrates how our culture has survived. "Houses" in the ballroom culture were created as locations for LGBTQIAP+ individuals to go when they didn't have a house. They had a family structure, replete with a home mother whose responsibility was to look after her children.

I wish my family and I had realized the varied statistics that many

LGBTQIAP+ youth fall into. The love I experienced at home could not be found in the other surroundings I had to deal with on a regular basis. They were as afraid of asking me if I was gay as I was of being "out." Even though they were aware of my sexuality, they made no effort to learn more about the LGBTQIAP+ community. In other words, they recognized queerness when they saw it, but not enough to teach me the intricacies and the risks.

Even though I was unfamiliar with my LGBT culture and lacked the resources to investigate it, I had a place to call home. Nanny made sure I had a place to call home. "Charity starts at home" was one of her favorite sayings. And I know that there are hundreds of other "Nanny"s all over the world who battle for tiny Black boys and girls, and gender nonconforming persons who are perceived as different. They recognize the indications and intervene to ensure that the youngsters know they are unconditionally loved. Nanny didn't keep her insights to herself. She instilled that in her children, who in turn planted that seed in us. They planted the seed in me to become a voice for other Black LGBTQ males who were unaware there was someone out there fighting for them every day.

There are many youngsters seeking support. Create the support network you want to have around you. I won't lie; this won't always be simple. I will not sell you the fable of "It Gets Better" like the media does without explaining how. The how comes from your willingness to take a gamble on yourself and build the support system you desire. I would also advise you to retake the campaign slogan and deploy it from a position of power. Tell people, especially non-queer and non-Black people, to "Make it Better." Things don't become better without action, and you have every right to request it.

The same way I grew up knowing I had a friend in Nanny, I hope Black LGBTQ males who will never meet me but will hear and see my words realize they always have a buddy in me. Sometimes all it takes is someone to see you for who you are. Nanny saw me, I saw you, and you now recognize yourself.

I recall a chat Nanny and I had later in life, just after I formally came out to her at the age of twenty-five. I'd always wanted to do it, but I didn't have the confidence till I was older. My fear was that being gay would disappoint them. Although they offered me no reason to believe so, the neighborhood I lived in was a different planet. One of HIV stigma and humiliation about gay sexuality. So I waited until I believed it was the appropriate time.

I was bawling on the phone, and she remained as calm as a rock. For starters, by confirming me in the moment and telling me that I didn't need to cry, and that being homosexual was not an embarrassment to my family. Second, she told me that she always knew and reminded me that "I love all my grandkids, and you know that I love you regardless." The last thing she said, however, is what will always stick with me: "And when you finally start dating a guy, you still gotta do just like all the other grandkids and bring him to meet me before anybody else."

Although that day has not yet arrived, it served as a reminder that, as diverse as we are as LGBTQ people, some things are simply universal, regardless of sex, gender, or (insert difference here). Elevating a community that is considered inferior to you to the same level of equity and equality affects only the oppressor.

Nanny will not win any GLAAD awards. She won't have her image on display during Black History Month, nor will she make headlines for working from a place of love. But because she saw me, I have the opportunity to tell everyone about her. And, just maybe, an LGBTQIAP+ person's family members or peers will read these words and absorb some of her soul.

CHAPTER 8
I SAW ME IN YOU

I'm going to write this in the only language I knew at the time—during my adolescence, before I fully understood transphobia and the actions that contribute to it. Knowing what I know now, there would have been no misgendering or switching between your birth name, Jermaine, and your chosen name, Hope. There would never have been this love for you while being afraid to be in public with you. Fortunately, despite our faults with you, our family only knew one way to raise a child—with love. So, despite our lack of education and resources to completely comprehend what was going on with you, we always loved you, and you found a way to love us back even more.

Oddly, my first memory of you was black and white. Every time I recall that initial meeting—from the parking lot to the benches, to everyone else—it's all in black and white. I'm not sure why my mind has done this with the recollection, but it could be because our lives as LGBT people have never been black and white.

It was a hot summer day, and I was probably around five or six at the time. We were all on our way to one of Nanny's renowned family reunion cookouts, which she used to organize with her siblings. We were a large family and most of us grew up within 30 to 45 minutes of each other. My uncle—the one I nicknamed "Uncle" and will learn more about later—always says, "Your cousins are your first set of friends," and he was absolutely correct.

I was holding my mother's hand as we stepped out of the car and started going toward the family—and there you were. You and roughly six other people were sitting on a picnic table, listening to a boom box and lost in thought. I remember I couldn't stop looking at you. I was a little lad at the time, coping with my feelings of difference. I stepped up to this table and noticed a reflection of myself. Even at that young age, I realized your group was "different," too.

Hey, Jermaine! " my mother murmured as we approached.

"Hey, Aunt Kaye." You grinned as you looked at me. You were a teen boy with a high-pitched voice that did not fit your physical appearance. I was just standing there, trying to digest everything.

At the time, you all had Jheri curl hair and wore tight, shredded denim trousers and even tighter tops. I listened as you gossiped like the women I used to see at my mother's salon. Except you were all boys, just like me. You had darker skin and had started wearing cosmetics by then. Your best friend, Corey, had lighter skin, a nice build, and the same high-pitched voice.

You were seated off on the side, away from everyone else, but it wasn't because you weren't accepted or welcomed in the place. You were all members of Nanny's sister's (my great-aunt Margaret's) crew. Nanny used to refer to you as "the Jersey City Crew," which included Great Aunt Margaret, her daughter Toni, her sons Rob, Paul, and Leonard, and my cousins Angel, Shawn, and you.

You admired my mother, and I could tell you were extremely close. I observed you and your buddies that day, too little to talk but old enough to listen. I couldn't stop staring at each of you. I mean, it was shocking because I was a youngster and had no idea what I was looking at. However, I knew that whatever it was you all were, I felt it and knew that something in me will one day be like you as well.

Even if I had G.G. He never discussed his sexuality, and he even brought girlfriends home to avoid any idea that he was gay. He was very closeted when I was growing up. That's why that moment in the park has always stuck with me. There is something to be said for the notion that you can't see yourself when you don't see other individuals like you existing, thriving, and working. I can only fathom how much guts it took for you to be yourself. Even though you had a secure house to return to, the world was not a safe place for people like you.

It's been years since you died, yet the world is still not a safe and accepting place for trans people. Some days, I feel it will never be. But the difference between then and today is that I strive to fight for people like you every day.

Throughout the years, I would see you at family gatherings with "the Jersey City Crew," and you would occasionally bring Corey along. However, every time I saw you, something changed. It began with the clothing. You began attending family gatherings in gowns. However, no one would ever make a disparaging comment.

Clothes came first, then nails and wigs. Each time I saw you, your voice and features became somewhat more feminine. From the slim young man I met that day in the park, you grew into the fun-loving, intelligent young woman you always knew you were. The woman I sensed you were from the moment I laid eyes on you.

I secretly wanted to be like you. When a youngster grows up with sentiments of both femininity and masculinity and little space to analyze them, he or she tends to reflect the best version of themselves. For me, it was you. I wasn't sure if I was a boy, a girl, or a science project, but I knew you existed, which meant I did as well, in whatever shape that could take.

It's story time again. Then I'll get back to chatting to you, my friend.

"Jermaine now wants to go by Hope," Nanny told us on the porch one day. I may have been around fourteen years old when we had this conversation before another of Nanny's famed family cookouts.

"Hope? " my mother inquired.

"Yes. Jermaine's name has changed to Hope Loretta Cureton.

The family exclaimed together, "Loretta!!! " It startled every bird out of the trees.

I recall someone saying, "Lord, if Loretta was here, she would whoop Jermaine's ass for that one." But then everyone started laughing.

I wanted to know who Loretta was. There was a brief moment of silence. My mother then added, "Loretta was Aunt Margaret's daughter who died at a young age of an asthma attack." "That is Jermaine's mother."

"Go in the house and get the picture album," Nanny instructed me. "I think I have a picture of Loretta." I dashed into the living room and collected a couple albums before returning to the porch. I handed her the books, and she began to read them, smiling as she flipped the pages, recalling all of her old memories.

"This is Loretta," she announced finally. It was a photo of my aunt sitting on a car hood, with my mother seated next to her. They had similar expressions and were both beaming.

"That damn Loretta was my best friend." My mom added, "We used to spend a lot of time together back then." That day, I learned that my mother was also Jermaine's godmother, which meant that if Loretta died, my mother was willing to accept responsibility for parenting him.

God-parenting is taken very seriously in the Black culture, and many of my family members attach legal papers to the title. Despite not having raised him, my mother spoke with Jermaine daily. She'd get him gifts for his birthday and Christmas. They were deeply in love with each other. My mother took her responsibilities seriously.

I recall her stating, "Well, if Jermaine wants to go by Hope, then we will call HER Hope."

Nanny scoffed somewhat at the concept. "I'm not calling him no damn

Hope. "That's Jermaine."

But my mother and her sisters just stared at Nanny with that "cut it the hell out" expression. My grandmother was old school, and while she loved deeply, she was averse to some changes. Partly because she didn't fully grasp what was going on. Partly because she saw the danger that society posed to people who did not fit into the norm, and she wanted us all to be secure regardless of who we were. But she was basically stubborn and just wanted things her way.

The Jersey City Crew showed up later that afternoon, as they usually did, with a case of beer, money to play cards, and a willingness to shit-talk. Hope came out of the car, and I exclaimed, "Hey, Jermai—hope."

She grinned and replied, "Hello, Matt!" Give me a hug, baby," so I did.

When Nanny first saw Hope, she made an expression. "What's with you not being Jermaine anymore? "

Hope said in joke, "Aunt Louise, I'm a lady, and I wanted a name that suited me. So I choose hope."

"You need some damn hope," Nanny replied. We all laughed hard at it, especially Hope. "Well, I'm going to call you Hope now, but I might call you Jermaine later. I've known you since you were in diapers as Jermaine, so it'll take some time now. "I am old."

Hope grinned and replied, "I answer to both Aunt Lou."

"Okay, baby, let me hug you," Nanny said.

Nanny always had a bite. She was obviously not someone who was more bark than bite. She just wanted to bark every now and then to get things off her chest. It was her way of digesting while still having her voice heard. It was a great day for us all. My aunts were all pumping Hope up with "Okay, Ms. Hope" and "I see you, Hope." We were bewildered and apprehensive, but also proud.

Okay, cuz, I'm back to handing you your flowers, so listen up. I was proud of your strength in making the decision to transition, knowing that society is not a safe place to live that existence. I wish I could have been as proud of my life back then, but I wasn't. I was concerned about what people would think if they saw me with someone like you. I was already dealing with enough hostility over my own sexuality. At fourteen, I wasn't ready to be in public with you.

But because of you, I was aware that I existed. I also knew by my early teens that I would not be transgender. But it also indicated there were others like me. Being queer is a journey. One that is always changing as previously hidden identities emerge. As previously hidden relationships gain prominence.

So my story goes like this: As a young boy, I was effeminate and assumed that I was intended to be a girl because I enjoyed lady things and had girl characteristics. That was all I could process from the age of five until roughly twelve, because I lacked a comprehensive language for gender and sexuality. My daydreams featured me as a girl named Dominique—after Dominique Dawes, the gymnast I longed to be.

My conviction that I was intended to be a girl had a strong correlation with my attraction to other boys. Girls liked boys. I didn't realize boys could like boys. At the time, the only experience I had with what happened when a boy liked a boy was watching my cousin transition.

It made me believe that I might be transsexual. I assumed that meant "a boy who wanted to be a girl" and that you were the physical embodiment of that. For long of my earlier years, I had the mindset that I would eventually change to a girl.

Everything changed for me when I was in high school. I had started sneaking Real Sex and Queer as Folk episodes. Although these shows primarily featured white homosexual men, they provided me with context for a society I was unfamiliar with, and representation to help me understand that I wasn't alone in my feminine nature.

My journey lead me to realize that I am gay. I developed from a boy who liked other boys to a guy who liked other men, and now I like many other identities. As I grew older, I became less concerned with precise labels and more in tune with what I genuinely enjoyed. My attraction to trans persons and those represented by the letters of the LGBTQIAP+ alphabet has prompted me to identify as queer. A term that encompasses all I am and want to be. The youngster who knew he was "different" now freely admits he is queer.

Then Hope, you knew I was different. While we never talked about it, you did little things to show it. "Always remember, Matt, CoverGirl doesn't CoverBoy," you stated at the BBQ. I laughed so hard as I watched you do your makeup before heading back outside into the hot heat. Your best buddy, Corey, was also present, but she was now known as "Cookie." You two were the funniest things at every cookout, and we'd all gather around to hear you tell stories.

The stories were always about your dating experiences, trips to the club, and whatever else you were up to. My mother was concerned because some of the stories discussed sex and other concerns you might encounter with males. There was always some narrative about how men wanted to mess with you, but only secretly. How you'd get wonderful gifts from men who publicly dated straight women, and then chuckle when you saw them out, since you knew the reality.

Growing up with transgender people in our family was normal for us, but it's not something I've heard from many other people. Nanny and my mother frequently claim that it runs in our family. When I think about the number of gay people in my family, I recall the debates over whether you are born queer or develop into it. The funniest thing of that argument, in my opinion, is that it makes no difference whether one is gay by birth or choice. Nobody should be able to change who you are. I'm glad our family never tried it either.

By the time I went away to college, I wasn't coming home as frequently, so I didn't see you until I was at the family picnic. It was always love, however. I'd even gotten to the point where I felt comfortable being in public with you. "Run me to the store, Matt!" " was your line over the years.

I had no idea why you always wanted me to take you to the store, but now I understand. You knew who I was even though I didn't, and that was our moment. Two spirits who truly understood what it meant to be different and the importance of having a space where we could simply be with one other. Laughing and laughing as we went to the neighborhood Walgreens to acquire your cigarettes—those damn Virginia Slims.

However, the laughs dwindled over time. Her visits to family cookouts were also notable. You had become "sick," as the family would say. Some claimed that breast implants leaked into your bloodstream. Some claim that it was the back-alley doctors who gave you poor hormone shots for all those years. Deep down, I believe we all understood what it was. An pandemic that continues to damage our people every day.

I last saw you at Nanny's place. You had recovered enough strength to get to the barbecue, but you couldn't go outside. You sat on Nanny's couch, but you had lost a lot of weight, so your face was slightly sunken in. I recall wanting to cry. I remember being afraid, wondering whether your situation might become mine one day. Even though we all knew the end was coming, you kept talking nonsense and telling those terrible jokes. We all sat with you and laughed and laughed. We knew it would be our final laugh with Hope, despite our hopes that you would live.

I was residing in Richmond, Virginia, when I received that call. In my mind, however, I knew you were gone. I had a dream about you that I had never had before. In Black culture, we frequently discuss how, when a person prepares to enter the afterlife, they begin to visit you in your dreams to have the conversation with you that they are unable to have in person. Our conversation the night you "visited" me was both simple and beautiful. You told me I was your brother and that you'd be OK.

The final story surrounding your death is one that I keep replaying in my thoughts. The family was summoned to Aunt Margaret's home in Jersey City. You lie on your bed, breathing shallowly but in excellent spirits. Family members and friends circled the bed and sat next to you. Nanny had had enough of the room becoming too loud due to the amount of talking.

"That's it, everybody, get out of the room," she yelled. Even though Aunt Margaret had been your main provider since your mother's death, Nanny glanced at her and stated, "You, too, need to leave! "And Aunt Margaret did.

Nanny pulled her chair to the side of the bed, looked you directly in the eyes, and said, "All right, Hope. This is your cruel aunt, Louise. I kicked everyone out of the room because they were so loud. "It is time for you to rest."

And now it's time to rest. A woman whose life had always been full of ups and downs, downs and downs, was finally able to lay her burdens down.

You taught me a lot about myself and confirmed that an LGBTQIAP+ community existed. You died during your early thirties. That's not okay.

Death has a way of bringing new life. I work very hard for myself and my community since I have witnessed personally the devastation of it.

A Blackness that cannot accept and defend queerness. A white society that seeks to destroy us all. You gave me hope by living and dying as the person you wanted to be.

I miss you a lot. Especially when I see your community being targeted for simply being. However, there is beauty in knowing that no matter which way I go, I was here and left as myself. I learned a lesson from you and your journey. Your tale will now live on forever in my words, so that everybody who reads them will know they exist because you did.

CHAPTER 9
CATCH THE BOY WITH THE FROG

"*M*attmole frijole, Mattmole frijole!" Daddy would reply when he noticed me walking through the house. That was his nickname for me. At the time, they referred to my younger brother as "Moot"—a moniker he gave up at the age of seven. If you know Garrett, you know that if he didn't like it, he would not let you say it.

I, on the other hand, liked it when my father called me "Mattmole frijole." He said it in a roaring voice that always made me giggle. As a child, my connection with my father was extremely straightforward. He was a manly man, although I was an effeminate child, so we didn't have much in common. He wasn't the type to hug, kiss, or tuck you into bed every night. But you always knew dad loved you, and he expressed it in various ways.

Christmas, birthdays, and vacations were the most obvious ways he demonstrated his appreciation. He never cut corners when it came to his children. My brother and I grew up in our parents' house. Our older sister, Tonya, and older brother, Gregory Jr., sometimes known as G.G., lived mostly on their own. Because they were so much older, they only lived with us for short periods of time while they were between homes. That was one thing about my father. No matter how much you messed up or irritated him, you could always return home. He remains like way to this day.

To comprehend my father and my relationship with him, you must first learn about his roots. My father was born in Williamsburg, Virginia, and spent his early years there. "A country nigga from the South," as he would describe it. My grandma claimed he was the first baby delivered at Williamsburg Hospital. As children, we would frequently visit the house where Dad grew up. It had been in the family since 1927, and was built on a tiny plot of land donated to my great-grandfather by the family for whom he worked. We used to despise those vacations, but they meant we wouldn't have to stay in Jersey for a few days, so we swallowed it up and coped with it. It was in the country, and there was nothing to do all day except relax and watch TV. My other grandma, whom we nicknamed "Grandma," lived there. She was my father's mother.

My grandmother's house was a shotgun house, and to the back right was another small shotgun house where my uncle Tick and aunt Lestine lived. Behind it, there were woods. I remember Grandma shrieking at us, "Y'all better get out of those woods!" Get a tick up in those hinepots!! " It wasn't until I was much older that I learned what mom was saying was rear parts, which is country slang for "your ass." "Hinepots" just sounds better.

To the back left of Grandma's was a much larger house. Grandma said her father worked the land in the 1920s. That the owner of the larger house handed her father the piece of land in front of the shotgun house. Her father built the house himself—a bathroom in the front, a kitchen with a bedroom to the side, a living room, and a dining room in the back, with a second bedroom to the side. If I wanted to go there now, I'd have to park my car where it used to be. All that history is now gone, as gentrification has turned the site into a parking lot. I believe it was because my father's family came from such modest origins that he never wanted his children to have the same experience.

The house was constructed in 1927, and Grandma was born in 1928. She and her two brothers were raised in the house. She went on to have three children and raised them in the same residence. That small house contained many memories, including several family members who died there. As children, we were scared to sleep in the rear room. It was always frigid, and you could see objects moving.

Yes. The house had ghosts, and Grandma would occasionally mention that she could see them. Television has a way of making you believe that everyone dies in a hospital bed, but in reality, many people die at home. Unless the circumstances required us to stay in the hospital, members of our family would prefer to die at home, surrounded by family and loved ones.

We were terrified to sleep in either of her house's bedrooms due to ghost stories. Then one day, Grandma questioned, "Why are you afraid of ghosts?" "

We immediately looked at her, like, "Because they are ghosts."

"Those are your relatives," she clarified. "Why would your relatives harm you? White people trained you to be terrified of ghosts. That is why they dressed in sheets like them. There's no reason to be terrified of ghosts of your own people." After she said that, I never worried sleeping in that house again.

Grandma was a strict woman. A God-fearing churchgoer who believed white people were the devil—and she used to say it proudly. She grew up when the world seemed very different. She was born in the South at the height of Jim Crow laws, a set of restrictions enacted by white lawmakers to dictate how "negroes" were to be treated. They were supposed to enforce racial segregation. Laws such as:

"No person or corporation shall require any white female nurse to nurse in wards or rooms in hospitals, either public or private, in which negro men are placed."

"No colored barber shall serve as a barber [to] white women or girls."

I'm sure she saw things I could never have imagined. My father descended from her and, as a result, inherited many of her traits. Strong and caring. You always knew he loved you, even if he wasn't always sure how to express it. Much like my relationship with my grandmother.

My favorite quote of his is, "Excuse the pig but not the hog, and catch the boy who got the frog." Dad would repeat it whenever he burped. His upbringing instilled in him many positive attributes, and some negative ones. He was somewhat patriarchal in his beliefs, and living with my mother, who is a very independent woman, must have been difficult for them both. They didn't fight or argue much in front of us, but he was clearly the king of his castle.

He would leave his plate on the table rather than emptying it, and he expected dinner to be prepared every night. That was part of his social indoctrination from childhood. Grandma would do that for him and her husband, Tuck. My mother has never loved the duty. Even though she would do it, she would tell him, "You can clean your plate off the table, negro." He would simply make a face and move on.

When I was a teenager, we went to Virginia. He and his older brother witnessed my then-seventy-plus-year-old grandma fry chicken, fix their plates, eat, and then clean up after them. I stopped her and told my father and uncle, "I know you're not about to have Grandma clean up after y'all."

They both looked up, surprised. Not mad at me, but they were so used to never having to pick up after themselves that they nearly forgot they were adults. They were scolded as children then. I cleared the table that day and let Grandma rest. I just stared at them like, "You n***** ought to be ashamed." My father sucked his teeth and said, "What? " He held his arms open. This was his standard reaction anytime he felt he was correct.

Grandma would continue the tradition established by her aunts and uncles before her. She, too, would pass away in that house, becoming the last to do so. I believe there's something to be said for dying on your own terms in your own home, with your ancestors present to take you home. She died surrounded by her children, right in the living room on the daybed I used to sleep on when I visited as a teenager. Her death was only the second time I'd seen my father cry; the first was when my uncle Rhem died in 2004.

My older brother, G.G., and sister, Tonya, have a different mother than Garrett and myself. My father was married to their mother, Sheila, for ten years until the divorce. He has been married to my mother for nearly thirty-five years. He's been married for over half his life. G.G. He moved to live with Grandma when he was sixteen. Garrett and I were really close to Nanny and G.G. and Tonya were considerably closer to Grandmother. Family dynamic.

G.G. He is six feet three, thin, and has darker complexion. He has the most exquisite teeth. We didn't grow up together, but by the time I was a teenager, he, Garrett, and I had formed a strong brotherhood tie. We went to the movies once a week and ate at Applebee's. We had lost a lot of time due to his absence earlier in life, but we made up for it throughout those years.

My dad and G.G. We had an odd relationship. It wasn't always horrible, but it was definitely not always good. They frequently butted heads. According to the stories I heard, my father married my mother, G.G. They didn't take it well. Typical stepmother drama. He and my father began to disagree while he was in his teens, so G.G. I went to live with my grandmother in Virginia. He would come back and visit from time to time, but our connection didn't truly take off until he was an adult and I was a teenager. We are 11 years apart.

Unfortunately, we wasted so much time. Had we been brave enough to talk to each other about how we were feeling, we might have discovered how much more alike we were than we realized. My brother, G.G. is gay. I believe that affected his connection with my father. Having a gay kid born in the 1970s who exhibited effeminate tendencies similar to mine was probably difficult for my father to deal with. There was far less LGBT visibility and representation in the 1970s than I had in the 1990s. G.G. She also had another mother, which contributed to her situation. Whereas my mother's side of the family was known to have LGBT members, G.G.'s mother may have struggled to know what to do.

A decade later, I believe my father would have approached my upbringing very differently. He had a second chance to make it right this time and have the relationship he desired with his oldest son. And I believe he overcompensated for me in ways he was unable to accomplish for G.G.

As macho as my father was, he simply let me be. If I wore something excessively frilly, he could use the term "sissy" every now and then. But he never flung the phrase at me, but rather at what I was doing.

My best recollection of him comes from a random day at Nanny's. I was approximately eleven or twelve years old and was outside playing football on my own, throwing the ball as high as I could and then catching it. He was just walking outside to take a cellphone call.

After he finished, my father approached me and asked, "Do you know how to play football?" "

I gave him the duh look and replied, "Yeah, I play it every day at school."

"All right, go out for a catch," he said. I handed him the ball and started sprinting. He took approximately five seconds before tossing it to me. When he watched me catch it, he had an expression of shock, followed by approval. He was even more amazed when I returned the football with a beautiful spiral. This was approximately the same time that I was demonstrating my natural athletic abilities to children on the playground. It's fascinating how both children and adults felt I couldn't do "boy" sports since I was more feminine.

My father was astounded, and I knew it. I believe he assumed that because I was the bookworm who showed little interest in sports, unlike Garrett, I didn't participate in them at all. I believe he saw G.G. multiple times. in me, and rather than resist what he was seeing, he chose not to interact with me at all.

That day altered our friendship forever. We stayed out there and played catch as the sun set. We went back and forth, with me running out for his passes, catching and returning them. Over and over again. That day taught us both a valuable lesson: we didn't have to be content with simply living in the same place. He wasn't going to like or understand everything about me, but it didn't mean he had to treat me differently. I discovered that I could have my father and maintain a relationship with him.

He began to take my interest in sports more seriously. He paid all my athletics fees. I even joined the high school bowling team, which was quite corny for a Black kid, and dad paid for everything I needed. The shoes, the balls, the fees—all of it. I could sense how much he had lost out on with G.G.

I was the only one of his children to attend private school, which he paid for. When I moved away to college, he covered my rent and a portion of my tuition each semester. He was willing to do anything for me.

However, this does not imply that our relationship was always ideal. As I became older and more self-sufficient, we frequently crossed paths. He assumed he could make judgments for me from over 300 miles away, which I rejected. I would phone my mother and vent. Sometimes her calls were filled with tears. My mother always informed me that my father cared about me. And she said it was difficult for him to accept the idea that I was my own person and that he could not make decisions for me as an adult.

I was about to become twenty-one when I received word that he had been hospitalized for congestive heart failure. His strength reflected his tenacity, particularly in terms of his own health. He feared hospitals and physicians, as do many Black families. Medical maltreatment and discrimination have made us skeptical of institutions accountable for our health. So we wait until we are nearly dead before we leave.

He was lying on his bed, barely breathing, when my brother Garrett went by and noticed him struggling. Garrett informed him, "I'll either take you to the hospital or call an ambulance." But any way, you're leaving."

We were going to celebrate my twenty-first birthday in Jersey, and I had brought all of my line brothers with me. I was in my final semester of college at Virginia Union University, and the party was going to be held in Plainfield.

About two hours before the celebration, I went to the hospital to see him alone. I just wanted to make sure he and I saw each other on our birthdays. I came into the room and noticed him sitting in front of the television, wearing a full-face oxygen mask. I'd never seen my father look afraid before. I'm not sure if he was terrified of how terrible his health had deteriorated or of seeing him in such a vulnerable state—the strongest man I knew suddenly reduced to a hospital bed.

I sat down with him for a few minutes, worried and scared to see him so ill. In that moment, all of our minor disagreements and head-butting seemed insignificant.

"I wish you could come tonight," I said.

"Yeah, me too," he replied. He seemed very disappointed. I believe he learned that being a sometimes selfish man comes at a cost. For me, missing this milestone was costly. I convinced him that everything was fine, and the most important thing was for him to get out of there.

I went that night to celebrate my twenty-first birthday with the rest of my family. My cousins, the village, and some of their friends all showed up to celebrate me legally becoming a "adult." It was a melancholy evening. I kept wishing my father was around me. It served as a reminder of how easily we take others for granted. It's easy to believe that you'll wake up each day with the same folks you were with the day before. You see them age, but do you see them growing old or imagine them not being here?

Something happened to him the day of the celebration. When I returned home a few weeks later for Thanksgiving, he appeared to be happier and more appreciative of life. We drank legally the first time. And when it came time to return to Virginia, he hugged me. It was so embarrassing I had no idea how to respond. I ultimately hugged him back and continued on my way.

The hug meant a lot to me because my father was not a PDA guy, and I had grown up to be the same. Even now, hugs from people I am only getting to know make me nervous. It's absolutely a barrier, as I learnt from him. His ability to change showed I could do it too. With that hug, I felt cherished.

Every day, I watch Black males condemn Black LGBTQ boys. That is not to suggest that my community is more homophobic than others, or that I don't see instances where Black straight guys confirm me, but it is not enough.

My father taught me that, while straight Black men are typically my oppressors, they can also be my guardians in certain situations. That the social conditioning that taught us to despise ourselves because of our gender and sex can be overcome. Much like my father, my community gets a second chance, one that allows their Black queer children to live in an anti-Black world that is already against them. I encounter bigotry everywhere else. My father ensured that I did not get it at home by using the instruments he had to the best of his ability.

CHAPTER 10
A SERMON IN NINE WORDS

*N*anny was never bashful about expressing her thoughts. She reached a point in her life where she was completely unfiltered—and given her life story, she deserved it. As previously stated, Nanny grew up as the youngest of thirteen children. When she was a baby, a house fire killed her two brothers and a sister. Over the years, she would lose more siblings. Despite being the youngest member of the group, she was always in charge. She had no idea how not to lead and did an excellent job of maintaining her position.

By the beginning of this story, we were all teenagers. Well, Little Rall, Rasul, and my cousin Thomas were. Thomas was my uncle Bobby's son who lived in Jersey City and used to pay us visits as we grew up. Thomas was always a pleasure to be around, and he always had an interesting story about what was going on in Jersey City's projects. He had now relocated to Plainfield and remained with Nanny. Garrett was about 10 then, and I was twelve or thirteen.

By now, we had left the "Big House" and Nanny had relocated to the other side of town, where she lived with my aunt Sarah and aunt Munch in a split-level house on Lewis Avenue—still in Plainfield. The house was not as large as the Big House, yet it functioned just as effectively. It had a large rear and side yard and was located in a peaceful area.

We met there after school, just like we did in the Big House. The teen years were intriguing for us because we didn't have much parental supervision most days. Little Rall and Thomas were placed in charge of the house, which meant that no one was truly in command of it. We would grab wine from the liquor cart and refill our bottles with water.

My aunts rarely drank the old stuff in the cabinet, so they never noticed. We'd watch improper channels on the cable box, curse, and do things we had no business doing. It was a house for puberty. When we began to grow pubic hair, the first evidence that we were "becoming men," we gave each other high fives and compliments.

Of course, it wasn't always like this, as my aunts and Nanny lived there. We only knew their schedules well enough to identify holes where the antics may occur. This became our home away from home, and I felt it was wonderful that we all had the opportunity to grow up as brothers rather than cousins.

My favorite moment at the new house was also one of the most significant life lessons I've ever learned, which I still practice today: how to care for my elders. It's something I wish more of us had learnt as children, especially Black children, who will inevitably inherit the duty when their parents and grandparents age.

We were downstairs in the den area, towards the back of the home. There was a hallway connecting the room to Nanny's room. Nanny cried, "Thomas, come in here really quick." Thomas stood up and began strolling down the corridor toward Nanny's room. He opened Nanny's door and let out the loudest scream—not one of fright, but more like "OMG!"

Sure, we are all nosy. I raced down the hallway and noticed Nanny standing there with her girdle, stockings on, requesting assistance to undress. I began to chuckle at Thomas's exaggerated reaction, and Rall looked away, laughing as well. But I was used to Nanny behaving like way.

Little Rall and Thomas had only recently returned to live with Nanny, so they weren't as used to assisting her as I was. I'd been assisting my grandma in getting dressed and undressed for years, so it was nothing new to me. For them, however, it was a surprise.

Getting Nanny ready requires a few things. She couldn't always snap her girdle in the back, so you'd have to help her do so. She was also a breast cancer survivor—twice—and had to have a double mastectomy, which involved removing both breasts. However, she was a warrior, and her battle scars just added to her confidence. She had some cones that she would use to fill out her bra. Sometimes I would help her.

So, we were all standing there, and Thomas said, "Nanny, put some clothes on. "I do not want to see you in your drawings!" She replied, "You'd better get accustomed to it. "You might have to wipe my ass someday."

We'd all lost it by this point. She was giggling, and we were all shouting with amusement. That is how it has always been with us. This was family, and despite being our matriarch, she was sometimes simply one of the boys. "Having fun with her grands," she would say. Eventually, the laughter subsided, and I entered the room to assist her in adjusting. I grabbed her coverall, which she would wear once she arrived home. I guess most people call them muumuus.

She thanked me and returned to bed to watch TV, while I went back into the other room to hang out with my cousins. We all laughed more as the two of them discussed how they would have to adjust to living with her.

"You might have to wipe my ass one day."

This was a sermon. These comments proved to be more powerful than anything I had ever heard from her at this point in my life, and I have carried them with me ever since. There is a lot of truth in those nine lines, and I'm not sure when a family should start talking to their children and grandchildren about how one day "the child becomes the parent." But that was the first lesson we learned, and I don't think we ever forgot it.

It reminded me of a similar situation in which I was not prepared for that role. When I was ten, my mother had her first brain surgery. I have vivid memories of the procedure, and the months preceding and after it. She survived the surgery, but the grownups did not want us to see her in that condition after the procedure, so we stayed with my grandma while she recovered. We eventually saw her a few weeks later, when she returned home. I recall her having staples on the side of her skull, and my eyes grew as large as quarters when I saw them.

She could tell from our expressions that we were terrified, but she assured us that she was OK. It was wonderful to have my mother back. But what are my responsibilities going forward? What did a 10-year-old know about caring for a parent? At the time, I wasn't doing anything for myself other than pouring my own breakfast and doing some housework. As children, it was not appropriate for me or my brother to take that position.

My family decided that it was not the appropriate time for the child to become an adult. My mother would be out of commission for more than six months, so my grandma and her church mates took it upon themselves to look after her. They cooked, cleaned, and ensured that we got to school every day. Nanny practically moved into the guest room to care for her. My family was always able to find a solution to any problem. Fortunately, my family made sure that we kids could remain kids.

However, by the age of fifteen, I would be expected to take on a greater amount of caregiving. Auntie Evelyn, Nanny's sister, would call on me to help her with her husband, Uncle Lester, who had a stroke and was no longer able to do much for himself. She would occasionally ask me to run errands for her and phone me to come watch him.

It was intriguing at first since my aunts and uncles all offered to watch him, but she refused. She clearly requested my assistance, which I gladly provided. I recall my mother checking in with me the first time, saying, "Are you sure you want to do this?" I informed her, "Yes, that's my uncle. I should wish to help care for him." She'd leave me off there, and I'd watch him for a few hours. Auntie Evelyn would pay me, and I would return home.

It never seemed to me at the time how large the burden was. Caring for aging people is certainly a blessing. They are our living ancestors, and what they did set the road for our existence. It's the least we can do to care for them.

Nanny truly meant we might have to wipe her ass one day.

On July 23, 2018, we all waited in the waiting room of Overlook Hospital in Summit, New Jersey. Nanny, just days before this, the physicians told you they discovered a tumor on your brain. It was a rare type of cancer called glioblastoma, and they would need surgery to remove it. I had just turned in this book, and the end of this chapter was written so differently. The saying you invented in jest so many years ago was now coming true.

I took a week off in August to come watch you while my mother and aunts were out of town. I was there to accompany you to your initial round of radiation and chemotherapy treatment. Every day, I cooked your breakfast and helped you dress. I measured your insulin and gave you three shots daily. I even helped you shower and changed the potty by your bed. I never didn't want to do those things for you. Here was the lesson you taught twenty years ago in action.

And now I understand why one chapter defines the entire book. You are the reason this book exists. There would be no stories, and I would not be here telling this narrative if you hadn't been there to guide my ship. To safeguard me throughout my childhood, youth, and adulthood. Even at your darkest and most terrifying moments, you informed me that your only regret was leaving us behind.

If the rest of the world could learn anything from you and this narrative, it would be that love is unconditional. That caring for someone who has taken care of you is one of the most powerful and transformational things you can do on this planet. Your saving me will allow me, my words, and our tale to save others, because storytelling is at the heart of it all.

I remember when I signed the book deal, I kept picturing myself at the book launch reading a chapter about you while you sat there in your Sunday best, beaming as always. I'm not sure if you'll ever see the end product.

However, the lesson learned before death remains valid. Despite everything I've gone through as a Black LGBTQ person, I still want to depart here with no actual regrets, just as you have. Although there are still memories to be made, I am confident that our final chapter will come one day.

I sat with you shortly after Christmas 2018 and we planned your funeral together. There were no tears, however. That was you. In your element. Controlling what you could still control. Your remarks that day were, "I've accepted that this cancer will kill me one day." I'm not saying I'm going tomorrow, but I do want all of my business addressed."

Cancer attacked one breast in the 1980s, and you overcame it. Cancer spread to your second breast in the 1990s, but you beat it again. Cancer spread to your lung in the 2000s, but you overcame it. Now it's in your head. A place where you cannot fight it. However, cancer is unaware that you are a Christian woman. So the joke is about cancer because one day you'll be in a position where it can't get to you again.

I have control over what is within my power. I'm focusing my energy on the things I can alter while praying for the rest. And, as you mentioned, I live my life without regrets. We still have time here together. And we'll keep the memories forever. Thank you.

CHAPTER 11
NO ONE ASKED, BUT I WAS WAITING

I was about 13 when it happened. It was Christmas and everyone was home. It was a normal night until the phone rang. Our cousins Rasul and Ral had gotten into a brawl at our grandmother's house. They were older teenagers, and they constantly managed to find an excuse to fight. Our aunts and grandmother broke up the fight, but you decided not to spend the evening there. You asked to remain with us, and my mother said it was great.

You were a cool relative, four or five years older than me. You enjoyed laughing, making jokes, and generally having fun. You had moved in with Nanny to finish high school and grow up with your other cousins. You were Uncle Bobby's only son, yet you two had a strained relationship. I didn't understand why at the time, but now that I do, it's helped me comprehend and think about you in new ways. You were well over six feet tall, with a medium-to-slender physique. You had darker skin and appeared gorgeous by most standards.

My mother left the house to go pick you up, while G and I waited eagerly for you to arrive. After you arrived, we played cards, watched movies, and kept the jokes going. We stayed up late that night, playing video games until it was time to sleep. We all went to bed in my and G's room. We had a bunk bed at the time, with G sleeping on the top bunk and you and I sleeping on the bottom.

I remember you began speaking to me, "Matt, are you awake? " I said sure, and you said, "Shhhh, you have to be quiet."

I remember G on the top bunk asking, "What are you talking about? "

And you're saying, "Shut up and go to bed!" " And everyone laughed.

You waited a few more minutes before asking me, "Matt." Are you awake? "

This time, I muttered, "Yes."

You then spoke louder, saying, "Garrett. Garrett! "

G did not respond. Garrett fell asleep quickly, and once he did, he slept soundly. You then asked me, "Do you feel that?" "

"Yeah." But I laughed and shouted, "Get your hand off my butt."

You laughed. "That's not my hand."

"You're lying," I replied. You then placed both hands on my hips while we slept side by side. Something was still poking me.

You were completely erect at this time. I was nervous. "We gonna get in trouble."

"You can't tell anyone, okay?" "You said. "Do you promise not to tell anyone? "

I promised. You then grabbed my hand, forcing me to touch it. It was the first time I'd ever touched someone else's penis. I knew it wasn't intended to happen. Cousins were not supposed to do these things with their cousins. But my body did not respond that way. My insides were doing something too.

It was the same emotion I got when I was seven and knew I was different. The 10-year-old who preferred to double Dutch rather than play football. Puberty was arrived, bringing with it the feelings I had always feared but yet desired. At the time, I understood that interactions and relationships could only exist between boys and girls. I never anticipated that one day I'd be able to explore the feelings I'd always had inside. Even when I daydreamed about it, you were not the person I expected to explore with.

We were touching each other now. I tried not to like it because you were my cousin. We were crossing a line that no family should cross. But it felt so right to a youngster who was constantly convinced he was wrong. Knowing that others were experiencing the same emotions reinforced everything I was feeling within. I knew it wasn't a hoax. However, the fact that we were doing it in private made me realize that no one would approve this. Particularly your girlfriend.

You then instructed me to get up and be extremely quiet since we were going downstairs for a few minutes. I was clearly nervous. You continued telling Matt, "It's fine. Trust me. You know I wouldn't do anything to injure you." Until this point, you hadn't done anything to harm me and were actually one of my closest cousins. I adored you. I knew you'd fight anyone who attempted to cross me. You were well-known for your fighting abilities since people frequently referred to you as gay although you had been dating girls your entire life.

I finally got out of bed, and you soon followed. We both carefully descended the stairs to my basement. Now, the basement was not like a cellar. It was a completely finished and rebuilt space with a large screen TV, couches, and a full bar. My family used to throw parties and gatherings in what we called the entertainment room.

You turned on the television, not too loudly, but enough that we could hear it. You tuned in to BET, which would play music videos from midnight to six a.m. It was approximately three a.m. We both sat on the couch to watch. I remained mute, still nervous. I had never done anything sexual with anyone before, although all of my school friends were talking about losing their virginity.

We sat for approximately 10 minutes before you finally got up. You then asked me to stand with you. At the time, you were at least a foot taller than me. You told me to take off my pajama bottoms, so I did. You then removed your shorts, followed by your boxers. You stood in front of me, fully erect, and said, "Taste it." I laughed and declined.

But then you replied, "Come on, Matt; taste it. This is how lads like us behave when we like each other." I eventually listened to you.

I knew it was wrong the whole time, not because I was having sexual relations with a man, but because you were my family. I only did that for about 45 seconds until you made me stop. Then you knelt down and told me to close my eyes. That is when you started having oral sex with me too. It was the oddest sensation in the world. Unfortunately, I didn't have a guide to learning sexuality as a queer boy. My crash course was unfolding right in front of me, and despite the shame I was experiencing, there was also joy. Something was happening to me that I couldn't describe. I was unaware that feelings and emotions existed.

After about a minute, you stopped. You then pushed me to the ground and climbed on top of me. You began humping me back and forth, but never penetrated me. It was simply our bodies on top of each other, back and forth for several minutes, as music played on the TV in the background.

Aretha Franklin was singing "A Rose Is Still a Rose." The irony of a song playing in the background about a young girl being deflowered and used by a guy. The irony of my laying on the cellar floor.

You eventually got up from me and told me to go to the bathroom because you wanted to show me something more. You turned on the lights and closed the door. You began to stroke yourself in front of me. I just stood there, nervous since I had no idea what to anticipate next. You said, "Just keep watching, Matt." So I stood there for a few minutes, observing you.

Then you started to moan faintly. I took a step back since I had no idea what was going to happen, and it did. You ejaculated in the toilet in front of me. I had no idea what sex entailed at the time, owing to my abstinence. I knew I didn't like girls that way, and the first question people would ask about sex was whether "you were fucking or not."

And I wasn't. We also received the bare minimum of sex education in school, so I was clueless of many things.

It was shocking to watch you ejaculate. I recall you telling me, "It's semen. One day, when no one is present, you should do this until you experience this feeling you've never had before and bust.

I looked at you and said, "I can't do that, I'm not old enough yet."

You laughed. "Matt, you're old enough. "Go ahead and try it."

By this point, anxiety had gripped me, and so many lines had been crossed that I finally exclaimed, "I don't want to do it."

"That is cool. Let's go to bed.

We returned upstairs and both went to bed. You rolled over to face the wall, as I sat there. For hours. I waited there till the light came up, unsure what to do or say, or how to face my parents. I eventually fell asleep in the early morning. I awoke later than you. You were still in bed behind me, watching television. I rolled over to gaze at you, and you replied, "Do you remember our promise, Matt?" "

"I won't tell anyone." I didn't. That night we kept our secret.

The secrecy surrounding sex seemed to become my norm. Two weeks later, I masturbated for the first time, and you were correct. I was old enough to have had what I subsequently learned was known as an orgasm. Despite knowing that what happened to you was terrible, I realized that I was definitely attracted to boys. I also understood that as puberty progressed, I would have to work even harder to repress these feelings. As a high school student, I was surrounded by sexually active teenagers.

So I suppressed. I was still the effeminate boy who could play sports, speak shit, and deal with minor bullying at the time. No matter how hard I tried, people could tell I wasn't into girls. But I still faked it, and

I was content with being a virgin. I wasn't prepared for sex, and my crash course made me feel bad instead than eager to attempt it with someone I didn't know.

Unfortunately, my faith would be broken again, and my will put to the test. This time in a high school restroom. I recall it was around one p.m. I had asked the teacher if I may use the restroom, just like any other time. I went up the corridor to the nearest one. Because it was class time, I assumed I was the only one in the bathroom.

I unzipped my pants and started peeing in the stand-up urinal in the corner. I sat there for approximately five seconds before I sensed someone approaching from behind me. At first, I froze since I had no idea what was going on. He wrapped his hands around me and slid down to touch my genitals. I felt every nerve in my body begin to tingle. I wasn't sure who was behind me, but I knew I was being raped.

I instantly stopped peeing, turned around, and shoved him away from me. It was a boy named Evan. We weren't pals, but I knew who he was. We were in the same grade and had previously taken classes together.

I zipped up my pants and exclaimed, "What the hell are you doing? "

"Yo, I am just playing. Evan screamed back, "Chill out."

"I don't play like that," I replied.

"Don't tell anyone, okay?" "

"I will not. Simply get out of here."

Interestingly, this was a boy who blended in with the popular kids, although most people suspected he was gay. Other classmates questioned him about his sexuality once, but he laughed it off and remained "one of the guys." This experience confirmed that he was not "one of the guys" and was most likely repressing his identity, just like I was. However, he was an assaulter. Furthermore, I learned that there were others like me concealed in plain sight. And, despite our efforts to conceal it, we could all see each other. Our mannerisms, our speech, and even our very beings exuded something distinct from the "norm," but we all strolled around in silence and concealment.

That restroom experience really turned me off from wanting to have sex with anyone else. It would be years before I even considered being vulnerable with someone. Thomas, I have realized that I shared a vulnerability with you. I was going to write about you based on my interpretation that night. From the guilty place. It seemed my innocence had been stripped. I now realize that this is not entirely accurate, and the experience has left me with more questions than answers.

If you were here now, I wouldn't hate you because I don't hate you anymore. I'd just ask, "Has anyone ever hurt you? Did anyone experiment with you sexually before you were ready? Who taught you about sex in a way you weren't ready to grasp, making you believe I needed to learn it firsthand from you so I knew who not to trust? "

I trusted you with my life that night because you promised not to hurt me. As disappointed and even angry as I was with you at times in my life, I now regret that no one was there to save you from whatever it was that you needed saving from. This is not to suggest that what you did was correct. It is to say that I now understand it from a perspective that is not based on my personal experience. I've established a space in which I feel empathy for my abuser—you—while also realizing that I've been wounded. I don't know for sure, but my intuition says you, too, were a victim. In turn, you made me a victim. Violence can follow a similar cycle. The night was gray, like your life. You were a great spirit and soul gone too soon.

I'll never forget the day I got the call that you had been slain while fighting for our cousin against some individuals who were threatening her. They called you "f*****," and you knocked them out one by one until you reached the third one, whose manhood couldn't bear losing to a "f*****," so he killed you. I recall that I did not cry. I was still hurt from that night and trying to understand what you done. I am glad I know, though, because I can finally mourn for you. The small child, like myself, wanted to be adored for his effeminate ways.

On September 11, 2001, I began my junior year of high school. By this point, I had become quite well integrated into the fabric of my school, so I was eager to return and begin the year. As a sophomore, I had participated in varsity track and bowling—no, there weren't many Black kids waiting up to bowl—so I was able to meet people outside of the Black friend circles I had built socially.

I was no longer a lower-classman. There was no more bewildered look when looking for a class. No more feeling scared among upperclassmen. I was officially a junior, which meant one step closer to being a senior, and one step closer to leaving Plainfield!!!

I left home in my usual attire. Short sleeve maroon polo shirt, gray dress pants, and gray Timberland boots—all of which are still at my parents' house now, because nothing is thrown away. I made a fast walk up Sloane Boulevard to Park Avenue's main roadway, then crossed the street, and arrived at my destination. Right in front of St. Mark's Church, where I had attended countless flea sales with Nanny on their front lawn.

Every day about 7:30, the bus would arrive. Then it was a fifteen-minute journey via the adjacent city of South Plainfield to Edison, traveling by the golf club and through the woods until we arrived. This vacation was quite typical for me during my freshman year. I didn't know anyone else on the bus, so I didn't have a "seatmate" or anything. It was just a typical uneventful commute from home to school and back every day, looking out the window and passing the time.

I now knew the bus routine and knew who would be riding with me. Instead of minding my own business, the first day began with gossip and small conversation. The usuals were present. My buddies Janae, Shombai, and a few others from the city. Then there was this boy.

I had never seen him in all my years living in Plainfield. His skin was light, and his hair was wavy. He was about my height and weight—at the time, I was five feet eleven and 145 pounds, dripping soaked with bricks in my pocket. I was quite thin. Because he was new on the bus, I figured he was a freshman. He reminded me of myself.

He sat approximately three rows behind me on the bus. I remember simply looking at him that first day. He looked at me, and I looked at him, but neither of us said anything at first. It was a strange feeling. It felt like I was staring at someone I'd known my entire life. His demeanor, his mannerisms—for the first time, I felt like I had met someone my age who was similar to me.

All my previous experiences included looking up to others, whether it was Hope or G.G. This was something more noticeable. This did not feel like the Evan situation. It was the moment I stopped feeling alone on my path. Kandi thought it was really Nene when they said, "WE SEE EACH OTHER." He was also attractive. Furthermore, he is still cute. (And he is going to read it.)

He was examining the rows to see who was who. He was minding his own business but also listening in on discussions around him to figure out what was going on. I wanted to know who he was, but I was not willing to go out of my way to ask. I was an upperclassman. And I was shy around boys until I got a good vibe from them.

When I first saw him, I felt awkwardly shy. That sense of being stuck—do I talk or not? I just sat. I gazed. Not a full-on gaze, but a glimpse followed by a look away. A stare, followed by a "Oh shit, he sees me staring," so I pretended I wasn't looking. Only to stare again, wondering who he was.

I felt heat surge up my neck and into my face, causing my head to sweat. I was stuck. I was already attracted to this kid. I, the boy who thought all he had to do was go to class, make excellent grades, and try to fit in until he could get out, was now confronted with his darkest nightmare. I was crushing.

The fifteen minutes on the bus that day felt like fifteen hours. I couldn't stop looking at him. I'd never been happier to get to school as I was that day. I recall rising up and rushing off the bus to find my pals.

I had my little girl group with whom I would hang out on a daily basis. Janet and Lee-Ann were my closest buddies in high school. We took several classes together and got along great. It felt fantastic to return to school and have friends I knew I could rely on. Women never asked me about my disabilities. They appreciated my one-liners, which I would become well-known for in my adult social commentary—I was essentially "reading" people before it became a catchphrase.

Unfortunately, I would never forget my first day of school for another reason. It was approximately ten a.m. We were in our third period classrooms when we heard an announcement over the speaker: "Students, please remain in your classes until otherwise instructed." The World Trade Center had been hit, and everything turned chaotic in the aftermath.

The next morning, the globe was shocked. It was as if I knew life had to continue on regardless of what happened the day before, but I had no idea what that meant. My routine remained the same. Up at 5:45. Shower. The long hike to Park Avenue. The bus arrived as it did every morning, and I boarded. There he was again. And there I was, staring at him and then looking down. I kept looking at him before turning my head away. The same routine as the day before, as if nothing had changed. But it did. On September 12, I finally got the lump out of my throat and spoke.

"Hi. "My name is George.

"Hey, I'm Zamis."

From there, we made small talk and learned a little more about one other. It was a typical getting-to-know-you talk. "What school did you attend before coming here? " and "Where in town do you live? "Very small talk—because my palms were sweating just from gaining the guts to speak. It was amazing to finally chat with someone who was similar to me—not overly macho or feminine. I suppose you could say I had "butterflies." He was simply a cool kid. I was simply a cool kid. In that moment, we were just two nice kids, and who we "were" didn't matter.

Zamis and I were rather close after that. We would see one other on the bus every day and perhaps converse in between classes. Because I was two grades above him, our schedules did not quite match, so there was little opportunity to form a lifelong bond. But what we had was sufficient for me.

Despite this, my crush did not go away. It was difficult for me not to regard him as a reflection. I realized he was probably suffering with some of the same issues about sexuality that I was. I only wish I had been strong enough to believe in that emotion and talk about it with you.

Knowing that someone is similar to you or shares your sexual identity is very different when neither of you are out. How do you just trust someone with the most important secret in your life? What if I told him I was gay and he claimed he wasn't? What if he told everyone at school about my situation? It was holding me back.

I did, however, come close to expressing it once. Before texting, GChat, and social networking, we all had AOL accounts and used AOL Instant Messenger. One day during my senior year, we just happened to be on AIM together. We started talking about how our days went and what we thought about school. Typical small talk topics.

However, there appeared to be some sort of inquisition taking place within the texts. He began asking questions about dating and the prom, eventually leading to the question that I had always dreaded answering. Then it came: "Are you gay?" "I recall seeing the message and feeling a scorching thrill run through my body. I did what I always did, and I answered the same way. "No, I am not gay. Are you in? "

"No."

I wish I'd said yes that day. I desperately wanted to say yes to him, but I knew I couldn't bear the thought of such a confirmation going public. I'd never told anyone about being gay. It was something I bottled up. Something I decided to handle on my own. But sometimes I wished the proper person had asked. a cousin or aunt. But the question never came. And would I even know who I should ask?

We remained buddies until I graduated and relocated to Virginia. He still had two years of high school to go, but I was more concerned about leaving New Jersey and whatever friends I had formed there. We had no communication after I graduated. It seemed better that way.

It would be over four years before I would see him again. I was twenty years old and attending my first gay pride weekend in Washington, DC. On the final night, a Sunday, I was strolling about looking for my pals. We were in a gay club, and LeToya Luckett had just done playing her new single, "Torn." She was a member of Destiny's Child before the group split up, but she is an incredible solo performer in her own right.

And there he was. Zae. Standing much taller and with a little more size. He grinned when he saw me, and I smiled in kind. We approached one other, hugged, and laughed over what we both knew but had never expressed. He looked quite good.

I remember speaking for a few minutes. I believe he had moved to Baltimore by then. I lived in Richmond, Virginia, about two hours from him. That was the nicest few minutes I had all year. We swapped numbers, pledged to stay in touch, and proceeded on our way.

All these years later, Zae and I are still friends. We occasionally converse on Facebook and make unpleasant jokes about each other in posts. Every time we talk, it feels like high school again. I sometimes wonder what would have happened if our paths had crossed at the proper time. If I'd been brave enough in high school to tell him how I truly felt. Or if I had been bold enough to follow him when we met in the club.

I guess we'll never know, but that's fine. Old ideas about what we could or could not have become have been replaced by new ideas about what we will be doing in the future.

Be bold, daring, and queer. I know it's easy to say, but much harder to do. I understand that some people will never be able to express their LGBT identity in that way for safety concerns.

Regardless of the hurdles, we have the potential to serve as a blueprint. We set the rules and define what our love will be for future generations. The confines Zae and I were placed into can no longer deny us the same rights, benefits, and access we deserve. We should have the same opportunity to express and promote our love—or, better yet, express and showcase ourselves.

Love who you want to love and do it without apology, including the face you see in the mirror every day. I deserved that type of affection. Zae deserved that type of affection. We deserved that type of affection.

CHAPTER 12
ALL THREE WERE ME

When "Pomp and Circumstance" started playing, I was standing right next to my best friend from high school, Janet Johnson. I'd heard this song previously while attending family graduations, but this time felt different. It was my turn.

Janet and I have known each other practically all our lives. It's interesting how we stood side by side as five-year-olds in a kindergarten class at Cook School, and now we'll be graduating together. My entire class began marching into the auditorium, passing all of our parents. I recall being very focused on getting things done and returning home to my family's BBQ. Nanny was cooking, and that was all I wanted from the day.

The graduation was like any other. Speeches by the principle and vice principal. The keynote speaker will read, followed by the valedictorian's address. I can't remember who our valedictorian was. But I still hear his voice. I will never forget how clumsily he concluded his speech.

"Congrats to all the graduates, we did this one for Tupac and Biggie."

At a Catholic school graduation, a white student made a reference to two murdered Black hip hop musicians. It was the same microaggression, the "I wanna be down" attitude that we frequently witnessed from white youngsters who wanted to engage in our culture. Today we call them "culture vultures."

All the white students screamed in acclaim and enthusiasm, while the majority of the black students simply groaned. It was the last time I wanted to deal with anti-Blackness at that institution. My culture was a joke to them the entire time I was in high school—something they could play with while never experiencing the persecution that its creators did.

After that folly, it was finally time to step onstage and receive my graduation. When they called my name, I received a good applause, much to the surprise of my relatives. Everyone assumed I was shy, but in truth I was far from it. The Matthew they had at home was nothing like the shady, gossipy George that many of my classmates grew to enjoy.

When the ceremony was done, we all went outside to take pictures. Janet and I took a few together as our parents talked. It was bad, too, because I was certain that this would be our last hoorah. Janet was going to Rutgers, while I was going to Virginia Union University. Important note: She and I are still excellent friends. At that age, it is easy to believe that time and distance might bring friendships to an end. It really does not.

Many people wanted me to stay in Jersey. Most of the children at the school chose to attend schools in Jersey rather than live too far away from home. Most people's lists included Ramapo, Seton Hall, Kean, Rutgers, and Fairleigh Dickinson. I, on the other hand, had enough New Jersey in my lifetime. I had determined a few months earlier that I was going to leave home and finally be myself, or what I imagined "myself" to look like.

I had formed the belief that my family, friends, city, and state were preventing me from expressing myself fully. That if I was away from all I knew and everyone who knew me, I'd be able to start over. New city, new acquaintances, and a fresh perspective on who I was. Finding my happiness. I was going to be like the individuals on Queer as Folk, living my adult life on my own terms while being "out."

My first choice was the University of Tennessee. Maybe it was because their school colors were orange, or because it was nearly a thousand miles from home, but I wanted to go. I received the financial aid package and was accepted before my mother put her foot down.

"You're not moving too far away. I'm fine with you leaving home, but you have to be somewhere I can reach you if something happens." I recall not being upset because I knew she was correct.

As far as I wanted to go, I was also terrified. I'd always been someone who took "measured risks," so traveling all the way to Tennessee to start my LGBT life seemed out of the question. I admit I would have struggled in a new environment at such a large school. Furthermore, I was prepared to dive back into a Black community.

The racial transition from middle to high school was difficult for me to manage. It's one thing to work with only Black children and worry about sexual identity. It's very different to deal with white kids because I'm Black and Black kids because I'm Gay. Double marginalization was a heavy burden.

Fortunately for me, my cousin had only started college the previous year in Virginia. Virginia Union University was a tiny school in Richmond with a rich history and a large Black population. It was one of the earliest historically black colleges and universities in the South.

This school was going to become my new home. Despite my desire to reside on campus, Gregory Johnson had other plans. Because my cousin was living down there and attending school, my father and sister agreed it was necessary to find an off-campus apartment. After all that running away from my family, I was going to be exactly back where I had started. But this felt different since I didn't have the same relationship with my cousin Stephanie as I did with Rall, Rasul, and my Jersey family. So it still appeared that this would be a fresh start for me. The apartments were directly behind the school and only a short walk from campus. The neighborhood wasn't great, but it wasn't terrible either, so my father, the cop, was fine with it.

Upon applying to the institution, I was awarded a partial presidential scholarship. This officially solidified George M. Johnson's decision to leave New Jersey. I was not leaving many friends behind, as I just had a few close ones. And by this point, we had all received cell phones, allowing us to communicate once I moved. I wasn't leaving family behind, either, because the city I was heading to contained my cousin, and Uncle and Aunt Crystal, who had moved to Richmond a few years earlier.

I was going to have the best of both worlds. Just enough family to make me happy. Far enough away from home for me to finally embark on my new adult journey. I knew I'd be living my adulthood outside of the closet. However, they remain in the closet. Let me clarify.

For some reason, I had convinced myself that I would be free. As if I was going to move to Virginia and be homosexual there, only to return home and be nothing. I figured I'd just have to go home for twenty days a year, so I could easily live my life in Virginia as a gay man and let my family find out later.

These were only dreams, of course.

The brightest spot that summer was when I first fell in love. Beyoncé was her name. The former lead vocalist of Destiny's Child was finally starting her own career. Prior to this point, I liked her but was not one of her biggest fans. I, too, blamed her for the split of Destiny's Child, a group I adored. After hearing "Crazy in Love" all summer and seeing her tear up the stage every time, I decided to buy her CD a week before heading to college.

Although I couldn't wait to get out of New Jersey, her CD provided me with a mental retreat. I would sit in my car alone and bash her.

Each song spoke to me. Her femininity embodied everything I felt inside. She was so feisty, sexy, and powerful. I wanted to be her. Not truly be her, but I would fantasize about her. I wanted to be myself, in Virginia, dancing to her. I wanted to be myself dancing to her.

My mother and Uncle Mack packed the truck and drove down the road to Virginia. I recall thinking to myself, "This was it." That the automobile would return home without me. My mother sat in the front seat. She remained mostly silent throughout the journey. Looking back, I can see what she was probably thinking. Worrying. Praying.

The youngster she had raised and safeguarded for so many years was about to be on his own. Just a phone call away, but not up that short corridor. No more track meets or running to pick me up from school. Her work was nearly finished, and she needed to figure out what life was like without her oldest child in the house.

On registration day, we arrived with almost 500 other youngsters. I expected it to be much worse than it was, based on all of the old episodes of A Different World I had studied before going down there. We had one issue with financial aid, but it isn't an HBCU experience until your financial aid is messed up at some time. We immediately sorted everything out, and I was properly registered.

We left college and went to the flat, which was literally two minutes away. I walked in and felt at home. I'm a seventeen-year-old with my own apartment. It felt like we were still living as adults. There's no oversight. No curfew. Simply living life.

We unpacked the vehicle and assembled my bed. My mother helped us put the apartment together. I remember thinking they would probably stay the night, but they did not. It was approximately six p.m. when she said they'd get back on the road and go up to Jersey. I could tell it was difficult for her to understand she was leaving me there. In that time, I was also afraid. I was actually doing it. I was truly escaping.

She grinned and added, "I know you won't be returning home after school." I laughed because she always knew me so well. She constantly recognizes me.

I was now in new terrain. I had Stephanie, but she turned out to be more of a homebody. She was also little older and had many other hobbies than mine. During those initial days, I had set my itinerary and was getting to know the campus a little better. But I could feel myself struggling.

In my head, I'd created a cosmos far from Jersey and everything I knew. One in which I would quickly make a new group of friends who had never met Matthew Johnson or George Johnson from New Jersey. But when I went to campus, I froze. I'd spent four of the most significant years of my life in a sea of whiteness, and my reintegration into Blackness was proving difficult. So I went to class, then home. Every day throughout the entire first week.

Then one night, while I was leaving to buy something to eat, I noticed my neighbor smoking a cigarette in front of the house. She cried. I believe she had just gotten into a dispute with her partner. I asked whether she was alright.

"Yeah," she replied. "I'm fine." She then inquired whether I had just moved in, and I explained that I was a freshman at Virginia Union. She chuckled, saying, "Oh, I go there too. I am a sophomore. "My name is Monique.

I introduced myself, and she added, "I realize you don't know me, but could you give me a ride to the store? " At that time, I agreed to any form of friendship.

I had no idea where I was heading, so she directed me. When we got into the car, I turned on some oldies. I always listened to them, regardless of who was with me. She smiled and exclaimed in a strong New York accent, "Oh shit, you like oldies, too!" "

On our walk to the store, I chatted about growing up in Jersey. She talked about New York and what it was like to attend Union, and we immediately became friends.

When we returned, she thanked me and went inside her apartment. I went to mine. It was late, so I decided to prepare for bed.

A knock on the door.

I looked at my cousin and inquired whether she was expecting someone. She shakes her head.

Stephanie peeked through the peephole and opened the door. It was the girl from across the corridor.

"Hey, Monique. I am your neighbor. We're over here with some food and drinks if you want them." My cousin smiled at me, and I agreed that we should go over.

Across the hall, we met Monique's boyfriend, Baron, her roommate Ivie, and their friend Tiara. Here I was, seventeen, drinking liquor on a school night without needing to smuggle it. No refilling liquor bottles with water. There will be no peeking over my shoulder for a parent. We sat there for hours, drinking and talking. It was around 3 a.m. I went back to my place to sleep before class.

They became my crew. Every night, we would gather together to eat, drink, and complete our homework. I had a car, so I became the designated driver for us all anytime we needed groceries, cigarettes, soda, or something to chew on. We formed our own small family unit. I even had a new nickname. Now I go by MJ. Monique offered me the moniker with Brooklyn bravado: "I dislike Matthew. I'm going to call you MJ." That was alright, but how are you going to say you don't like my name?! I still giggle about it.

However, it was around this time that I became closest to Tiara. We were inseparable. She was a heavyset girl with brown skin from Northern Virginia. We used to bike everywhere together. When it came time for homecoming, she and I decided to go to the shopping to get our costumes. We were listening to music on the way when she asked me unexpectedly, "Are you gay?" "

My heart suddenly fell to the floor. I dealt with the same stupid question and assumption in K-6, middle school, high school, and now college. I looked at her and replied, "No, why would you believe that? "

"Oh, I mean, your mannerisms and such come across as queer. It's okay if you are.

I simply glanced forward and replied, "Yeah, I'm not."

There was no mystical waking. The fresh Virginia air did not provide the boost of valor I had expected. There was one boy who had always been afraid of the ramifications of coming out.

Tiara's question made me realize something new that day. I longed to be perfect. To be right. To follow society norms.

As much as I wanted to live an openly homosexual life, I also didn't want to disappoint. Even with the limited knowledge I had gained from the media's portrayal of homosexual people and my personal experience, I understood being gay was not something to be applauded. Coming on campus felt like more of the same: questions that came out as invasive and untidy, never from a place of genuine concern.

It was slightly depressing that I had planned for so long to have my moment and was still unprepared for it. We frequently see coming-out tales. Some better, some worse. We don't see what happened before that time. How many times did a person try to push through that barrier to reach that point?

Throughout this chapter, you'll notice my fluctuating levels of confidence and despair. Notice my bewilderment about how strong I was in some instances and how weak I was in others, since that is exactly what coming out is. It is not the end. It is something that is constantly occurring. You have to come out somewhere all the time. Each new job. Each new city you dwell in. Every each individual you meet, you will most likely have to explain your identity.

I wanted to be gay on my terms. I didn't want to stick out too much. I wanted to be able to feel macho while being gay. Being so visible as gay was the problem. It was something I couldn't control, and there was no grace period to accept and make my own—I couldn't put it off till eternity like a school debt. That is, whether or not I embraced it, people would call me gay. Some of us are pressured to accept an identity before we are truly ready to do so.

I recall returning to my apartment that day, went straight into my room, and closing the door. I put Beyoncé's Dangerously in Love on the CD player and lay on my bed. It was a pleasant September day, but I did not want to be outside. I wanted to be alone. Just a few weeks into my new existence, the escape plan I had worked on for so long was shattered in a single conversation. Matthew was a sissy. George was a prick. MJ was gay. All three were me.

There is an ancient saying that says, "The thing you are trying to hide is usually what you give off the most." For all those years, I thought I was hiding something, and it was the most evident thing people knew about me as soon as I entered the room and spoke. That day, I knew I couldn't escape who I was, since I was going to be myself whether I liked it or not. So I laid there. I listened to Beyoncé on repeat. And accepted that one day, my answer to the inquiry "Are you gay?" The answer would be "Yes."

Just not today.

CHAPTER 13
CROSSING, NOT CHASING

I was depressed at the beginning of second semester. I'd made friends, gotten a 3.1 in my first semester, and was having a good time, but deep down, I despised myself. I woke up everyday and was still not the person I wanted to be. I wanted to have pals, good grades, and parties, but as a gay person. Not like this guy, who was terrified of having sex for fear that someone might find out. I was depressed without knowing what it was.

So I basically gave up. I gave up going to class. I gave up trying to come out as gay. I felt empty and feeling nothing. During that semester, I acquired a part-time work at Ruby Tuesday and made decent money. When I got home, I'd meet up with Baron and our friend Syd to smoke pot and play hoops. I was smoking up to three blunts per day, working, partying, drinking, and not attending class. I was what you'd call "smoked out," and it showed.

By the conclusion of the semester, I'd failed two classes, passed one, and had an Incomplete in another. My GPA fell below 3.0, and I lost my scholarship. That summer, I called my mother and informed her I was considering moving back home permanently. I assumed I knew what she was going to say: "What time do you want me to come fetch you? But she didn't. She explained to me how I had to tough it out and find it out on my own.

That summer allowed me to refocus. I'd always been smart. I had always received good scores, and I had forgotten how joyful they made me feel. That first year, I was so preoccupied with discovering myself outside of the confines of my house that I lost touch with the aspects of myself that I valued. I liked being a bookworm. I like being considered the smartest person in the room. I shouldn't have strayed from these things.

I returned to school the following semester, more driven than ever, to right the wrongs of the previous one. The first was my cannabis habit, which had become out of hand. Purple haze, as it is known, was my favorite vice. The drug made things seem less genuine. All the depression and rage I was experiencing. The weed also allowed me to be in a room with people who didn't mind that I was masking my sexual orientation. It was my masculine coping strategy. All the hood boys smoked, as did I.

I reduced my pot usage from daily to once every couple weeks. Being high all the time was no longer my thing. I wasn't even chasing the environments that involved it. I wanted to control my vice rather than let it rule me. My days became quite straightforward after that. I would go to class in the morning, work at night, and return home. Do my assignment and repeat. It wasn't ideal, but it worked for me. I still got to be MJ to the gang, George to the college, and me to myself.

Then one day, as I was heading home, I heard a huge ruckus in "the Square," our common area, which is similar to what people call a quad. It was spring of 2005. Spring was always a significant time on HBCU campuses due of the Divine Nine. The Divine Nine are the nine Black Greek Letter groups based on the ideas of Christianity, chivalry, friendship, sisterhood, brotherhood, and the fight for Blackness. These groups included some of the finest leaders in modern Black history. Becoming a member was practically equivalent to becoming campus royalty.

I had my eye on a specific male organization that a friend of mine happened to be a member of. As I proceeded nearer the crowd, I realized there must have been at least 700 students gathered around Delta Sigma Theta Sorority, Inc.'s newest recruits. The Square became hysterical. People cheered and screamed. I had no idea what I was witnessing at the time, but I was completely captivated by everything.

The throng grew louder as the girls marched through the Square, arms linked together, chins resting on one another's backs. They marched to a specific location in the Square before the Dean—the organization's leader—ordered them to stop. The older sorors then urged that the audience be quiet.

The Square was a redbrick patio area situated directly in front of Henderson Center. Henderson was a two-story structure that held the nurse's office, cafeteria, administrative offices, and a bookstore. During campus parties in the Square, the brick walls would practically "sweat" as the alcohol poured out of our pores while we danced.

"UNLOCK," the Dean demanded.

The girls spread out across the Square shoulder to shoulder, arms in front, elbows to the side of their hips, all facing the crowd. I stood and watched in awe. The girls waited until their Dean directed them to address the college.

I was standing in the back of the throng, just tall enough to see over everyone. The sorority dressed red and white, and all the girls' faces were covered with masks. There were individuals in front of them, issuing commands. The girl in front would hear the command and pass it on to the girl at the end. She'd make a squeak to indicate that she had received the message. It was like witnessing the most intense game of telephone I'd ever witnessed.

When an order was successfully passed, the girl in the front position would instruct the rest of the girls on the line to speak. They would announce some information to the entire campus. When they finished one call-and-response, they moved on to the next piece of information. It was very Black in spirit and tied to Black American culture. It was a performance that exemplified how Black people have always built their own venues when refused admittance to society by white culture.

We weren't allowed to join white Greek fraternities and sororities, so we not only formed our own, but also personalized it.

All of the kids were cheering on their pals, holding balloons with numbers that corresponded to where the females were waiting in line. This went on for over an hour. I later learned that the ceremony was known as a probate, which is the introduction of new members into a sorority or fraternity. They "spit" facts and history, stepped, and exchanged greetings with the older sorors by altering the lyrics to popular songs and replaced them with phrases that spoke to the person being praised. It was one of the most electrifying things I'd ever witnessed.

During the same semester, I befriended a guy named Lawrence who was in the same business program as me. He was short, with darker skin, and one of the sharpest persons I had met up to that moment. We had also been assigned to a campus quiz team dubbed the Honda Campus All-Stars. It was essentially like Jeopardy! but against sixty-four other HBCUs around the country. Every year, they flew us to Orlando, Florida, to compete against one another.

Lawrence and I became close colleagues and eventually became great friends. I recall our friendship being odd since he was from Detroit, had a strong voice, and was very macho. My sexual orientation, however, was never discussed. He would be one of the few people I met who wasn't obsessed with finding an answer to that question.

As we grew closer, I discovered that he was also a member of the college fraternity Alpha Phi Alpha. I saw him out and about with the brothers on school or doing community work, and I became increasingly interested in what a fraternity could offer me. Masculinity—or, more specifically, my lack thereof—was always on my mind. Joining a fraternity sounded like a win-win scenario.

Fraternities were founded on masculine ideas. Lawrence's fraternity had "Aims," which included "manly deeds, scholarship, and love for all mankind." Manly stood out to me. It was a stark contrast to the sororities' femininity.

I decided I wanted to join Alpha Phi Alpha. I had high grades, was attractive (or so I believed), and would be an asset to the organization if picked. I also understood, based on tales around the yard, that networking was as much about getting online as it was about being the ideal applicant. It was all about who you knew and how well you demonstrated your interest by attending fraternity events and making yourself known.

I saw the fraternity as an opportunity to take on leadership responsibilities and be a part of a larger movement. I was also hoping for brotherhood, which meant being able to form platonic bonds with other guys. For me, joining a fraternity meant getting the one thing I had always desired: a male ideal tied to me.

Lawrence and I discussed it occasionally during the spring and summer of 2005. But it wasn't until fall 2005 that I told him I wanted to join the group. After that, I didn't hear anything about it, so I kind of let it go.

Then, at the start of the next semester, I received a phone call from an unknown number around 9:30 p.m. "Hello, might I speak with George please?" A guy inquired anxiously.

"This is George."

"Well, my name is Charles, and I think I am your line brother."

By this point, I understood enough about fraternity life to be unsure whether this was true or a hoax. My heart fell. I'd heard awful stories about pledging, and while I wasn't a punk, I didn't want to walk into a setup or an ambush. We talked on the phone for a few minutes before he told me where I was going to meet him.

I informed my two cousins that I had been called about being online. They glanced at me in disbelief. I gave them the address and phone number of the person who called me. They told me to text when I arrived at my destination and again on my way home. This was going to be our system to keep me secure.

I got into my car, nervous as hell. But I put on my trusty Anita Baker and went to the other side of town by myself. I recall arriving at the apartment building and standing outside. I called first before entering because I wasn't sure if this was a joke or not. I still wanted to be part of the band. But after hearing about how people had been maimed and even murdered due to hazing, I was on high alert while I waited. Eventually, one of the line brothers came out to greet me.

We then entered the flat, where there were eleven other guys, some of whom I knew and others I had never seen on campus before. That night, we got to know one other. Some people were thrilled to meet me. Others were irritated because they had to catch up to the "new boy". Apparently, they had been meeting up covertly since the semester prior. Although they weren't formally "online," they had been organizing study groups to go over the information the brothers had given them during the holiday break. So, despite being added before the official start of the process, I was already behind on the stuff I should have studied.

Either way, I was ecstatic. I was finally doing something that contradicted all I had previously known. This was my search for masculinity, and I was finally going to be able to show how tough I truly was. Masculinity seemed necessary. I was drawn to it in other males. Gaining masculinity almost felt like an act of self-love. I wanted to like myself. I wanted to fall in love with myself.

We all formed strong bonds throughout the three months we spent online together (back then you could say that, now you had to say "membership intake process"). We were required to meet on a regular basis to review material. Then, regularly, share this knowledge with siblings. We don't typically talk openly about what happens in private, but I can state that it is similar to many past customs.

Prior to 1989, pledging was considered "aboveground," meaning that the boys and girls on line were visible to the public. They would meet throughout the day on campus and follow the fraternity brothers and sorority sisters around. They would act on demand for the entire university to see. It could even include humiliation, but that was all part of the process.

Unfortunately, in 1988, someone attempting to join Alpha Phi Alpha (the same fraternity I was interested in) was killed in a hazing episode gone awry. To assist prevent this from happening again, a federal anti-hazing statute was adopted, and most states now have anti-hazing laws. However, for the past fifty years or so, at least one person has died every year during a hazing in the United States, mainly due to alcohol consumption. These deaths have resulted in jail time, fines, and penalties for all organizations and individuals involved. Due to my initial reservations about meeting my line brothers and the possibility of a pledge process—as it is not an unwritten need for everyone.

Burning Sands, a film released in 2017, portrayed the cruelty of pledging for those going through the subterranean process at an HBCU. The described method is common for many people and reflects numerous historical traditions. Although the film did not tell the entire story, it did depict some of the myths and truths of the pledge process.

Throughout the intake process, we were becoming more than simply friends. We were becoming a fraternity, almost like a family. I never had a "clique" growing up. Joining the brotherhood meant I'd have a lifelong relationship with these individuals.

During that time "on line"—a term no longer used because to its hazing connotations—there were many highs and lows. There's also a lot of fussing, fighting, and arguing. However, we were all growing together. Some of us were really manly, while others were not so much. But it didn't seem to matter. This was the environment I had longed for. One in which my feminine nature did not matter and people saw me for who I was. I discovered that among my line brothers.

Our admission process began in January, when we learned about the fraternity and met with the brothers on a regular basis to discuss it. We were studying all this for a variety of reasons. First, we needed to understand the organization's history. Second, to proceed with national intake, we must pass the national test. Finally, we would have to convey much of this material to the campus in a show format that included stepping and greetings to elder brothers and sororities.

We attended national intake in March. It took two weekends and was an all-day event each time. We met with senior brothers from our advisory chapter on weekends to go over the same things we had been learning in secret for two months. Because of the subterranean procedure, many people on campus were aware of what was going on but pretended not to know. After we all passed the tests, our probate was scheduled for April 7.

During the period between the national test and the probate, we had to communicate with older brothers from our undergraduate chapter. This is a custom that occurs when you approach the end of your journey. We were all training at my apartment one night when my older brother contacted me and, of course, asked me the same question I had been getting my entire life. He was on speakerphone when he blurted out, "I heard you were gay. We do not tolerate that f***** stuff in our chapter." My first response was, "I am not gay, big brother, and I understand." He hung off the phone.

My line brothers stood silently around me. I was angry. And when I'm upset, I do what I usually do. I started crying. My line brother Gerald was the first to approach me. He stared at me and drew me in for a hug. I burst down crying even more. "I'm so tired of being called that."

The rest of my line brothers eventually came up and hugged me. "Tough it out," some of them advised. "We have come too far." They were correct.

To be honest, I never intended to drop out or give up. When kids said I wasn't tough enough to play football, I proved them wrong. I'd spent my entire life proving people wrong. Because people questioned my sexuality, I wanted to make sure I worked harder than a straight youngster under the same conditions. I wasn't there to be equally good. I went there to prove I was better.

That night, some of my brothers hugged themselves because they were also concealing their queerness. Together, we formed a much stronger one. I understood that no matter what occurred next, these eight men would always have my back.

Finally, April 7th, 2006 arrived. Our fraternity was founded in 1906, and our chapter was established by a fraternity founder in 1907, making it one of the earliest chapters in Black Greek history. I was seventh at the line. Our fraternity's gem number is seven, as we have seven founders.

When we arrived on campus, there must have been a thousand people waiting for us in the Square. We locked up under one another's shoulders, chins on one other's backs, masks on, and marched into the Square, or so I imagined. There was another test, of course. Our older brothers put blindfolds over our masks. We then resumed marching, with the Ace's arm resting on our Dean's shoulder, who was now our eyes.

I recall feeling incredibly nervous. In addition to it being nearly 85 degrees outside that night, this was the moment we'd all been waiting for. We marched till we came to a sudden stop. My heart was thumping quite quickly. I realized we'd plummeted. "Deathmarching," as it is known, is difficult to perform blindfolded. We got up and continued. We then walked down some stairs and around the corner, stopping again. We were commanded to unlock, and they removed our blindfolds.

The light of Alpha appeared before us. It's literally the Alpha symbol in lights. Everyone was getting us excited for the concert. Despite my anxieties and perspiration, I felt stronger than ever in that moment. Our Dean hollered to lock up one more time, and we were out again. This time, we removed our blindfolds and began our final march to the concert.

When we arrived to the Square, the crowd surged. My Dean called for us to unlock, so we did. I looked ahead and saw my entire village. My mother, Aunt Sarah, Aunt Munch, Uncle, cousins, Monique, Ivie, and everyone. Everyone yelled at the top of their lungs, "I SEE YOU, NUMBER SEVEN!!! "

I felt seen, not for my sexuality, but because I was finally at the top of a Black societal pyramid. I was no longer the kid who worried about being chosen last. I was no longer being forced into something male to defend myself. I was defining my masculinity. I was the focus of attention for a good cause. Everyone was rooting for me.

We spent about two hours that night doing a concert for the campus that featured greetings, history, and stepping. Because of an unusual thirty-minute thunderstorm, our probate began in the Square, moved inside to a large room in Henderson Center, and then returned to the Square. While inside, half the line removed their masks and introduced themselves. When we got back outside, we started again. Travon was standing in front of me, and I could feel my mouth dry as terror gripped me. Despite my fear, I realized I had fought too hard to waste this opportunity.

When they got to me, the audience erupted. In that moment, it didn't matter if I was gay to my older brothers, who had questioned me throughout my journey. It didn't matter how they thought about me; I was tough enough, like everyone else. Black Greek life in our community contains symbolism. It shows how tough you are. That you "crossed the burning sands" and lived to tell the tale.

That night, I demonstrated to myself that manhood is not a single entity. That there was a version of manhood, a version of "manly," that looked like me. It was now up to me to represent Black queer people. I wanted to be the person who future Black LGBTQ people could look to for guidance on how to establish their masculinity on their own terms. I went into everything with the intention of pursuing masculinity. I came out understanding there was nothing for me to pursue. That the only thing left for me to do was be this person, but with all honesty. It was time for me to open out about my sexuality and sexual space while also being a member of Alpha Phi Alpha.

CHAPTER 14
THE FIRST TIME WAS MINE

I never fantasized about sex with another boy. When I did think about sex, I imagined a girl having sex with a boy. In my head, I invented Dominique, a female version of myself who would have sex with any of the boys I fantasized about. That was the one thing that ever made sense to me, until it no longer did. College opened my eyes to a few things.

As I already stated, there was no mainstream gay representation back then, and my high school taught sexual education in a very outdated manner. The whole "birds and bees" discussion never made sense to me since who cared about how birds and bees mate? Sex education was a total joke, and the fact that we were in a Catholic school didn't help. We addressed abstinence as the ideal contraception, of course. They used graphs and charts, and that awful banana, to demonstrate how to properly apply a condom.

We learnt the fundamentals of sex. What an erection is, what sperm does, and how it gets to an egg to make a kid. We studied about sexually transmitted infections (STIs) such chlamydia, gonorrhea and HIV. However, this is just the surface level of knowledge. There is no mention of how these illnesses disproportionately affect one community, particularly HIV in the black community.

Nor did we learn about sex between guys. I focused on masturbation rather than sex, mostly because I couldn't envision having sex with anyone else. I had feelings for boys, but the only encounters I'd had with them—Thomas and Evan—were not like the ones I'd seen in love stories or pornography. These were largely between men and women, and they were enthusiastic and confident in each other. The pornographic stories were overly idealized, but the emotion was present. Even the clichéd plots were better than my actual experience, which involved no romantic love at all. So sex with myself would have to satisfy until I was able to trust myself around someone else.

That moment for me did not occur until my junior year of college. I stayed a virgin until I was almost twenty-one, which was unusual in our family. It had been difficult to lie about having sex (with a girl) to all my heterosexual cousins. I'd never seen a vagina except in the movies and had no desire to.

Being a member of a Greek Letter Organization can put you in the spotlight in college, exposing you to a whole new group of people who were previously unaware of your existence. One boy in particular took a liking to me and requested my phone number. At first, I assumed his desire was platonic. He was a friend of someone in my chapter, so I assumed he was simply being social.

As we began texting each other, the discussion swiftly turned from cordial to X-rated. This was great with me, except I wasn't sure who was supposed to be who in the bedroom, or whether it would just play out. I didn't inquire since, to be honest, I didn't know what the terms were. He waited until his roommate was out of town one weekend before inviting me over.

When I arrived, he had already prepared dinner for both of us, which was cool. We talked briefly before moving to the couch to watch television. After approximately twenty minutes, he moved closer to under my arm. This suggested to me that I would have to be the more "dominant" person in this encounter—based on what I had learned from observing girls interact with boys.

We cuddled for a few minutes before I leaned in and started kissing. This was my first time kissing a boy. I recall being incredibly nervous in that time since I had no idea what I was doing. I wasn't sure where it would lead. I only recall quiet. I know it felt right. It was the first time I shared my body with someone on my own terms. In that moment, I felt like I had agency.

He eventually came up for air and said, "You're a really good kisser." I was surprised, since it was my first time, but I was also too enthusiastic to care and went back in for more. As we kissed, he began to unzip my pants. In this point, I realized he wasn't new to this.

He reached down and pulled out my dick. He promptly rushed to give me a head. I just sat back and enjoyed it, as I could tell he did. He was also clearly seasoned in his field, as seen by his confident demeanor at work. He then approached me and asked if I wanted to try him. I said yes. I started, and he cautioned, "Watch your teeth." I didn't want to show him I was inexperienced. So I slowed down, took my time, and thankfully settled into a good groove. He had no idea I was a virgin, so I did my best to appear dominating like my favorite porn star. I was an actor and this was my film.

My body was filled with a rush of exhilaration. This was far greater than loosing my virginity. For once, I consented to my body's sexual pleasure. This moment also reaffirmed that I could have sex as I wanted. And that it might be passionate and kind, but above all, enjoyable and rewarding. His body felt amazing in my mouth.

I got up after a bit and kissed him again. We both got up and went into his bedroom, where we stripped absolutely naked. He removed his clothes and instantly lay on his stomach. I then pulled off my shirt and boxer briefs. I got behind him. There was moonlight shining through the drapes of the dark chamber. Two Black boys under the blue moonlight. How poetic, and should I say ironic?

I was afraid as hell. One, because I had no idea what I was doing, whereas he certainly did. Two, it was still college, and I was afraid that word would spread that I was inexperienced or bad in bed, which would have been a campus rumor. Let alone the fact that I was having sex with a man and someone from my chapter.

For the first few minutes, we dry humped and grinded. As we kissed, I was behind him, stomach on his back. After a few minutes of fun and games, he stood up and walked to his nightstand, where he took out a condom and lube. He then rested on his stomach. I knew what I needed to do, even though I'd never done it before. However, I just had one point of reference: seven years of watching pornography. Although the pornography was heterosexual, it served as a sufficient reference point for me to complete the task.

I recall the condom being blue and tasting like cotton candy. I poured some lube on him, got him on his knees, and started sliding in from behind. I tried not to force it because I feared it would be difficult; I didn't want this moment to hurt. So I eased in gradually till I heard him moan.

As we moved, I could tell he was excited; I was, too, but my pride warned me not to show it. I felt in control and pleased of myself for getting it perfect on the first try, despite being scared. I wanted to maintain my dominance in that moment. We went at it for approximately fifteen minutes before I began to feel the sensation. Feet are weak and waist is numb. I finally arrived and let out a loud moan, to the point that he requested me to be quiet for the neighbors. I pulled out of him and kissed him while he masturbated. Then he came.

That night was magnificent. I overcame a fear and had sex with a man on my own terms. Years of repressing my identity and refusing to date or kiss had all culminated in one magnificent night in an apartment on the outskirts of Richmond, Virginia. I did not want to leave, and he did not force me. However, I got up to call one of my line brothers. I left a voicemail informing him that I had finally had sex.

I then returned to his bedroom and slipped beneath the sheets. We lay naked in one other's arms that night. For him, I was nothing more than a cute frat boy on campus. For me, I had finally begun my voyage of sexual exploration and couldn't wait to do it again.

He and I had sex again two weeks later, when school ended for the summer. He went home, and I remained in Richmond. That summer, however, I did not do it again. I had numerous sexual encounters that included mutual masturbation, kissing, and playing around, but I couldn't bring myself to have penetrative intercourse again.

I was hesitant because I still had many questions. As much as I enjoyed being in control, I wasn't sure whether I always wanted to be the dominating person in the bedroom. I was still inexperienced with sex, much less with gay culture and sexual positions. I wasn't sure if because I "topped" him meant I had to constantly be at the top. I also wanted to try the bottom position, which I equate with being more submissive. (Though, if you know me, that has never been the case.) I simply wanted time to contemplate and determine whether sex for me would be a casual hookup or if I was ready to pursue anything more.

The next semester, I began my final year of college. I was promoted to fraternity president and became one of the most well-known students on school. It was a tremendous start to what promised to be a fantastic year. By then, I was using Black Gay Chat, an online dating app.

One night, I received a message from another boy who attended school with me. He explained that he had always had a crush on me and wanted to meet up. It was the night before my trip to Jersey for my birthday, so I decided to meet up with him as an early birthday gift to myself. I arrived at his residence, and we both began drinking while watching television. This continued around five minutes until we started kissing and undressing each other.

He then rose up, took my hands, and escorted me to his bedroom. We took each other's clothes off quickly yet deliberately. Then he urged me to lie on the bed. He instructed me to "turn over" while he put a condom on himself.

My heart immediately began to rush. Nervously, I asked him what he was doing, and he answered, "You." I laughed at first, but then informed him that I had never been on the bottom. He glanced at me and said, "Well, that's about to change tonight."

I was so nervous. There is some fear, as with most first-time experiences. But this was my ass, and I was having trouble imagining someone within. And he was... huge. But I was going to try.

I had previously topped someone who plainly enjoyed it, but he had been having anal sex before I came along. He knew what to anticipate. I did not. As an enthusiastic porn watcher, all I knew about anal sex was that it was painful, or at least it was portrayed as way on camera.

Nervous and intoxicated, I listened and sank to my stomach. He climbed on top and gradually inserted himself into me. It was the worst pain I'd ever experienced in my life. He then put more lubrication and tried again, which felt marginally better. He started his stroking stroke. Eventually, I felt a mix of pleasure and pain.

I can't say I didn't enjoy it; I did. But it was definitely painful. In those few minutes, however, I can say he was gentle. His intention was not to hurt me, and mine was to make him happy too. He didn't stay inside me long, thankfully. He kissed me before pulling away. I didn't stay long, and I didn't masturbate afterwards. I was in shock. I just wanted to go home.

The next morning, my line brothers and I were organizing a trip to Jersey for my birthday, and I had to drive. However, I was in pain. I informed them what I had done, and before we left, they picked up some Tylenol for me and said, "It will take some time to get used to it." They were proud, however. I'd gotten another gay badge of distinction, like it was from the Boy Scouts or something.

I was in pain for over three weeks after that encounter and was frightened to go to the doctor for help since I would have had to admit to having anal sex. So, like most other traumatic experiences in my life, I swallowed it up and suffered with the pain until my body healed. I did not have sex for months after that incident.

But, after a while, I had the courage to try it again, this time considerably more prepared. With each experience, I learned more about my body and had the ability to say, "No, that hurts." Sex should be enjoyable. And there are safe ways to ensure this. As they say, practice makes perfect, and I eventually got enough of practice.

I frequently wonder what my first sexual encounters would have been like if I had been able to learn about queer sex at the same time that my straight friends and classmates did. My queer sexuality, like the rest of my queer life, was a huge, dangerous crash course.

There is a significant risk in not offering good sex education to children, particularly those who have sex outside of heteronormative norms. Sure, we knew about HIV, but in a school full of white students, it wasn't a priority. Despite the reality that Black queer people are at the biggest risk for it, receiving sex education via a white lens made me believe I was as invincible as my white classmates.

The "banana test" demonstrated how to correctly apply a condom while none of us had a banana between our legs. Being taught sex as a means of reproducing offspring rather than as a kind of pleasure deprived me and others of the opportunity to properly understand what we were getting ourselves into. I put myself in danger because I had no idea what I was doing and lacked the tools, resources, and supportive community to gain that information.

The risk factors for LGBT persons engaging in sex remain higher than those of all other communities. We are more susceptible to sexually transmitted infections. The CDC has previously estimated that 50 percent of Black men who have sex with men will develop HIV over their lives. A quarter of Latino homosexuals will also get the virus. Denying the queer population a basic sex education as teenagers perpetuates the prevalence of these numbers.

Because of this deprivation, many queer people experience a second adolescence for the majority of their adult life. During my adolescence, I didn't experiment with sexual behavior. I didn't have openly gay friends or mentors growing up. I did not have the opportunity to date boys or have a relationship. I had to figure a lot of this stuff out on my own. So, when I entered adulthood, I was only beginning to understand about the mistakes people make and the lessons they acquire while exploring in their teens. We suppress who we are throughout our formative years, when we should be learning and growing alongside our straight peers and with the protection and support of our family. Our society's heteronormative systems have the ability to affect the course of our life.

Losing my virginity twice altered my perspective of who I was and how I could interact in a relationship. If you allow yourself to be forced into a box created by society, you will never know what you like or who you are. Learn what you enjoy and dislike. Create the ideal sexual environment for you. Sex, regardless of gender or sexual identity, is an essential component of human development. Nobody has the right to deny us the resources we require to properly interact with one another.

I wish I knew what you know now. But I don't regret any of my sexual encounters. And to be honest, this was the scariest chapter for me to write. Because this chapter requires a level of vulnerability with the outside world that I'm not sure I'm ready for. My first experience was very enjoyable. My second experience was quite painful. But I went through it and shared it, so you may not have to.

Will this aspect of my story be met with opposition? Absolutely. But I'll be damned if I don't tell it out of dread. My greatest fear is that queer teenagers will be left to experiment with their sexual experiences. It's worth my embarrassment if it means you're all better prepared.

CHAPTER 15
I BURIED KENNY, AND I WAS REBORN

It was Christmas break, and I was preparing to return to college for my final semester.

"Be safe on that road, Matt," my mother told me as I prepared to go. "Make sure to contact or text me when you arrive home. And make sure you tell your father goodbye."

I strolled down the corridor that I used to run up and down as a child to their bedroom. "Are you out?" He asked.

I loved how he said it. He was always startled that I was leaving, although I had been out of the house for nearly four years. I sometimes think he wished I hadn't had to go to return to Virginia. I only got to see my father a few times a year, and as quiet as he is, he is incredibly family-oriented.

That holiday had been wonderful, as it had always been for the previous twenty-one years of my life. Full of relatives, and full of presents. My father was always meticulous about completing all the tasks on the list and more. We celebrated Christmas dinner with the entire family, with Nanny taking the lead on the cooking as usual. We sat for hours watching the NBA, eating food, drinking alcohol.

But I also despised being in Jersey. My memories are largely of times spent with family, a few with friends, and many alone. Jersey was a constant reminder of how much I felt alone. Virginia, on the other hand, was my current life. I had formed a close circle of friends with whom I would spend every day. I had fraternity brothers, specifically my line brothers. They'd become the new constant in my life. Text messages are sent daily, and phone calls are made nightly. We were all joined at the hip.

During the break, we were all messaging and contacting each other, discussing how we got what we wanted and didn't want. On Christmas, I contacted one of my favorite line brothers, Kenny. He lived in Philadelphia. We were the only two people on the line from the north. We had a very special relationship. Things were simply different up north. The flair, the street life, the music—we both got it.

He finally received the camera he'd been wanting all year. I remember talking to him on the phone, and he was so enthusiastic about that camera. Kenny and I used to travel home together during breaks because I had a car and Philadelphia wasn't too far from Plainfield. That day, we were discussing if he would accompany me back home, but he wanted to stay for the full break. I had to return to Virginia early since I had a job to get back to.

I spoke with all my brothers that day. For the first time, I felt like I'd found my happy medium. The child who had struggled to make friends for so long now had a whole gang of individuals he can call brothers. It also helped that, paradoxically, I ended up on a line with four straight people and four gay people, as you'll find out later.

It was such a fitting metaphor for my life. The balance between being straight and queer. My battle to fit in any community. It was the space I'd always needed—the one that proved I could live and prosper in both. I did not had to compromise my identity to please others.

I was pleased to be returning to the life I had built with these young men. It was December 28, not too chilly outside, but with a slight winter chill. It was approximately ten a.m. I finally got on the road. I remember this day vividly since it was also the first time my father got out of bed to see me off.

My mother would always see me off to school. My dad would usually yell, "Are you out?" " And I'd say, "Yeah." He'd add, "Aite, be safe," and that was all. This time was quite different. He walked up to the door. It was the first time he had hugged me in my adult life. I recall feeling strange when he said, "Be safe," as he always does. But I knew he was changing for the better. Perhaps he realized how difficult this day was going to be.

I got on the road and drove down the Jersey Turnpike. I used to listen to Black R&B music from the 1960s, including my favorite, The Best of Anita Baker. I'd be in the car with my two vanilla donuts and Dunkaccino coffee, with a backup Sprite, listening to Anita. It generally took me almost five hours to get to school.

Anita's voice was booming through my speakers. And I was singing as loudly as I could. Hit all the notes on one of my favorite songs. That's when I got the idea to contact all my brothers. I figured having somebody to talk to would make the five-hour ride go much faster.

So, I began with my Ace Wayne. We talked for about thirty minutes before I moved on to Charles. Then Gerald. Then David. Then Kenny...

Kenny had a street-smart attitude, was never afraid to fight if necessary, and wore a full-face beard like most Philly residents did at the time. Despite his harsh exterior, he had a golden heart and an infectious sense of humor.

Kenny never had money, and being online was pricey. So, during the process, I footed the tab for various items we needed to make for the elder brothers or for ourselves. He was roughly a year younger than me. I was a caregiver at heart. I looked at Kenny the same way I did for Garrett, my younger brother.

We enjoyed the same music and could relate from a family standpoint. He also had a license but no car, and I despised driving everywhere, so he was the ideal person to give the keys to. Kenny drove my car so frequently that he may have been covered by my insurance. We studied together frequently, and when he had his "blow up" moments, I could always pull him back in. It felt like we had grown up together.

When I was driving back to Virginia after school breaks, I would pick him up in Philadelphia, swap to the passenger seat, hand Kenny the keys, and fall asleep. Kenny enjoyed driving. Those road excursions are what I remember most.

After I finished talking with David, something came over me, and I told myself, "Don't call Kenny right now." Wait until you get home to call him." So I passed over Kenny and called Travon, with whom I gossiped for two hours as usual. Dimetrius came next, followed by Kris. By this point, I was in Virginia, about 40 minutes outside Richmond. I was almost home when my phone rang.

I glanced and realized it was Gerald, which puzzled me because I had previously spoken with him that day. I took it, but all I heard was screaming. Just screaming. I said, "Calm down; what's going on?" "

"Kenny is dead, Kenny is dead."

I didn't instantly respond with emotions, but rather with clarifying questions. "Who told you this? "

"David called me and said that he is dead."

Now, I knew David had a buddy or cousin named Kenny, so I was very positive that was who he was referring about. "Let me call David." I quickly contacted David and put him on speaker while I was still driving. "So, what's going on?" "

"Kenny died in the morning. I called to talk to him about Christmas, and his cousin answered the phone and told me he had died."

I recall falling down in tears. I kept thinking why I didn't call him that day. Perhaps the cosmos simply knew I needed to be closer to home when I received that news. I called my roommate, Travon, right away and informed him that Kenny had died and that I would be home quickly.

Death was not among the traumas I had endured in my life up to that moment. I'd had great-uncles die before, but I'd never lost someone close to me. This was an emotion I wasn't sure how to handle. I recall arriving at the apartment and finding two of our friends, Ari and Cine, comforting Travon.

I went to the window and called my mother. I had to inform her that I had arrived home and also tell her what had happened to Kenny. She could tell I wasn't doing well the moment she picked up. And I could hardly say, "Kenny died." I remember her shouting, "WHAT! " She instantly pulled herself together and apologized to me. She knew I'd never been through anything like that, and her sole worry was that I was okay.

My line brothers were not simply random members in my family. My entire line came home with me for my twenty-first birthday party. There are photos of Kenny and my grandmother dancing together that night. My line brothers are my family. I was hurt, as was my family. Not only did they know Kenny, but they also realized it could have been any of us.

She prayed with me by phone. That was usually our go-to when I was in a crisis or in need of mending. Prayer was always the method for me to find peace during the hardest times of my life. I recall finally calming down and hanging up the phone with her. She said she'd check in on me and let her know about everything that happened that week.

Within hours, my entire line had arrived at my flat, having traveled from DC, Virginia, and Maryland to be together. We got intoxicated, just like any group of twenty- and twenty-one-year-olds would. There was much love in the room, almost enough to offset the tragedy we were experiencing internally.

That week completely transformed my perspective on life. I was our chapter president at the time, so I handled the most of the arrangements for Kenny. We had a memorial at school. For the first time in years, a student died on our campus. Kenny was beloved by many. We also arranged a memorial service for him in his hometown, as is customary in our fraternity when a brother passes away. Many of the brothers present said they had never witnessed someone so young die.

The week following Kenny's death seemed to pass in slow motion, leading up to the ultimate moment. The funeral was difficult for us all. That day was about finality. But I didn't want to let him. I was asked to speak on behalf of the fraternity before a church packed with over a thousand people. One of the most essential sections of my speech was about how, if a world can have marvels, it must also have sorrow.

We regularly discuss miracles and how they happen. How there is a path out of nothing. However, we rarely discuss the contrary, the devastation that is left behind. We must cherish the memory of a person who is no longer with us. The things we wished we had spoken.

That last one offended some of my line brothers, particularly those who were queer. They felt they never had a chance to discuss it with him. They had no idea that Kenny and I had already discussed that topic. He died knowing everything about each.

We were on our way to the mall, just me and him, the summer before, when he began to query about us—the line brothers he felt weren't straight. "Are you gay, George?" But this time, I didn't respond in the same manner I normally did. Something about Kenny told me it was okay to tell him the truth. I took a big breath and answered, "Yeah."

By this point, I had already come out to other line brothers who identified as gay. My coming out to them was slow. The first person I informed was my line brother Dimetrius. He claimed he'd reveal me a secret one night while I was staying at his flat. He showed me a picture and a card from his boyfriend who lived in Washington, D.C. Dimetrius and I had become close, and he felt he could discuss this with me.

I saw him and admitted I was gay too. This moment was very important to me. I was officially making gay buddies. Until this time, even if I had gay friends, we didn't discuss it. I was trying to stay safe on campus. So now, knowing that I was gay, I had someone who was more than just a buddy, but a line brother to whom I would be bound for life. That felt like returning home.

He then started teaching me about the community and telling me which of our other line brothers were also gay. I would finally meet them and tell them the truth. So, perhaps it was because I had practiced with others that I felt more comfortable telling Kenny. It was still new to me, though, because I hadn't discussed my sexuality with any of my hetero line brothers—or any hetero person, for that matter.

Kenny looked at me and said, "Okay."

I recall thinking back, "Are you sure you're okay with that?" "

He had a huge laugh and added, "Nigga, I don't care about that. You're my brother, and I'll always have your back." I'd heard and seen horrific stories of individuals coming out. Whether it was as public as Ellen or my gay line brothers informing me about their experiences.

That day, we sworn each other to secrecy and talked about all the stories about our line, including who was gay and who wasn't. This happened before I had a clear grasp of what "outing" meant. Looking back, I realize I should not have done that. I should not have stated anything about anyone else's business because it could have serious ramifications. At the time, I was more concerned with our line being completely clear to one another, but it was a foolish decision on my behalf. Especially since it has always been a source of worry for me.

It was my first experience being myself around individuals who society had told me would never accept me. The individuals in my own community, whom I had been taught to fear, could look beyond my identity. Kenny was only 19 then. And for a person of my age, growing up in the hood, who had no problem with my sexuality? That was a miraculous event in my life.

That miracle had become a tragedy. I almost finished my speech that day, but I was too overwhelmed by my emotions. I paused in the middle of a fraternity prayer and returned to sit close to my line brothers, who were also grieving. We made it through the funeral and headed to the cemetery, where we said our final goodbyes. Kenny's parents agreed that we should be pallbearers, and since there were exactly eight of us, it seems that the cosmos did as well.

We formed a line on each side of the casket according to our numbers. My line's Ace yelled out the commands, and we started walking toward his tomb. We all stood there as the reverend recited the final burial prayer. "Ashes to ashes, dust to dust," he said, and I remember feeling numb. I believe we were all numb. We were both young and enduring loss. As we stood side by side, we began linking arms without realizing it. I believe it was the only way for us to avoid falling apart.

I recall them lowering him to the ground. I just stood there. People were leaving, but I didn't want to leave. I did not want that to be our last memory. I wanted it to all be a dream. So I stood there, looking at his casket in the ground. A friend eventually came up and remarked, "It's all right, George." "You can let him go."

We spent the rest of the day with his family before heading back on the road later that afternoon. The automobile trip back was quiet. We were all exhausted, left with only memories of our departed friend. It felt like the entire world was watching us grieve, and all we had to rely on was one another. When we returned to Virginia, that is exactly what we did.

Death pulls people together. His loss was unbearable, and as is common in the Black community during times of trauma, there was no processing. There was no therapy or healing. It was time to return to school and restart our lives as if the catastrophe had never happened.

An elder brother noticed us suffering with this one day and drew us all away, telling us to remember these words forever: "You never completely get over death. It just gets easier to deal with every day."

I've been carrying those words for almost a decade. I've had the thought of dying for nearly as long. For me, death that day was more than Kenny's absence. There was also a death within me. A death that many of us experience when we lose someone who loved us completely. Death is not just a physical body leaving the earth.

As a Black LGBTQ person, I have died numerous times. Will most certainly die hundreds of times before my bodily demise. That is the lesson of death, though: from death comes rebirth. A renewal in thought, processing, and life.

I remember being known only as Matthew Johnson and how important that youngster was to so many people until he wasn't. His death has been slow, but ever-changing. Matthew's death was necessary for the birth of George.

More significantly, I needed to let go of all I had been taught about my identity to thrive on my own. It wasn't about becoming this version of "George" or "Matthew" or "MJ" anymore. It was about accepting that whatever you named me or how I identified, I had to be good with it. I witnessed what it was like for people to be "slowly dying" because they never got to be their true selves.

That day I buried Kenny and the notion that I would always have time. I'm sure Kenny too felt he had more time. Time and death are far closer than many of us want them to be.

I should have phoned Kenny that day. He was alive, and even if I couldn't reach him or received horrible news, I should have called. I think about all the times I've procrastinated "the call" throughout my life, only to discover that sometimes that call never comes. Time waits for no one, and for Black LGBTQ people, there are far too many people attempting to steal our little time. So live your life.

Five months after Kenny died, I graduated college. It was the pinnacle of my life then. My family traveled down to Virginia. The entire hamlet was present to witness my graduation. All the aunts, uncles, great-aunts, and grandmothers were beaming from ear to ear.

After that, I was seated next to my mother in the backseat of the truck my family had driven down. She grabbed my head, lay it on her shoulder, and murmured, "I'm so proud of you." I didn't back away. I just laid there. A woman with her son. She frequently worried about the boy. She did everything she could to safeguard the boy. The boy was formally maturing into adulthood.

My college graduation was a celebration not only for myself, but for the entire village. It was a celebration of all the years they had to see my development from a young, shy, effeminate boy to an adult. They were able to celebrate their aspirations and dreams via me, someone they helped construct, something some of them were unable to achieve on their own. The village obtained a college degree.

At twenty-one, I understood what it was like to desire to be in love with a boy. I know what it was like to suffer the most devastating loss in your life. I knew both delight and sadness. I knew both victory and trauma. Most importantly, I recognized the path that remained ahead of me, with many more difficulties to overcome and barriers to break down. And, while I had lived a full life, I realized I still had a lot more to live.

The contents of this book may not be copied, reproduced or transmitted without the express written permission of the author or publisher. Under no circumstances will the publisher or author be responsible or liable for any damages, compensation or monetary loss arising from the information contained in this book, whether directly or indirectly. .

Disclaimer Notice:

Although the author and publisher have made every effort to ensure the accuracy and completeness of the content, they do not, however, make any representations or warranties as to the accuracy, completeness, or reliability of the content. , suitability or availability of the information, products, services or related graphics contained in the book for any purpose. Readers are solely responsible for their use of the information contained in this book

Every effort has been made to make this book possible. If any omission or error has occurred unintentionally, the author and publisher will be happy to acknowledge it in upcoming versions.

Copyright © 2025

All rights reserved.

Printed in Great Britain
by Amazon